THE
SHEFFIELD
UNITED
MISCELLANY

THE
SHEFFIELD
UNITED
MISCELLANY

DARREN PHILLIPS

First published 2010

The History Press
The Mill, Brimscombe Port
Stroud, Gloucestershire, GL5 2QG
www.thehistorypress.co.uk

British Library Cataloguing in Publication Data.
A catalogue record for this book is available from the British Library.

ISBN 978 0 7524 5718 5

Typesetting and origination by The History Press
Printed in Great Britain

INTRODUCTION &
ACKNOWLEDGEMENTS

S heffield United's fortunes may fluctuate, but over the past century or so the Blades have been, and will remain, one of football's biggest names. The city famous for its steel production is possibly just as renowned for its sporting heritage. And rightly so.

United fans have seen many interesting times. Some great ones too, not to mention some superb players. In this book I have attempted to show some of the most fascinating events and names to have shaped life at Bramall Lane.

Charting the history of a pioneering club and one of the Football League's first great teams has been a great pleasure for me, and one which it is to be hoped readers will draw equal delight from.

Onto more practical points. Although the author gets his or her name on a book cover and praise or brickbats for their efforts, the end product is usually the fruit of many people's labours. A host of others will usually play a quiet but highly significant role. The process of writing this book was no different and this is my chance to pay due respect. Although the thanks to follow will be brief, they are no less heartfelt because of that. A debt of gratitude is due to all at The History Press for their professionalism, but especially to Michelle Tilling for her help and understanding throughout the writing and editorial process. I would also like to thank Peter Charlton who, during his editorship of the *Sheffield Star*, encouraged me to write my first words about the Blades.

FOUNDING FATHERS

Except for the odd football match, Bramall Lane was mostly used by the Sheffield United Cricket Club. But an FA Cup semi-final between Preston North End and West Bromwich Albion in March 1889, which raised £558 1s from the 22,688 in attendance, convinced Charles Stokes, a junior member of the cricket committee, that forming a football club to use the ground regularly alongside its existing occupants would be a good idea. It was a sporting endeavour he felt would go down well given its popularity elsewhere in the city. Also, with the ground's original 'soccer' tenants Sheffield Wednesday to quit, it kept the presence of a football team. Just as importantly it would earn money during the winter months, so in March of the same year Sir Charles Clegg, president of the Sheffield FA, balloted his fellow committee members. They accepted his proposal by a single vote mainly due to the assistance offered by more established local clubs. However, that pledged support was withdrawn. Sheffield FC were first to pull out of the venture and were swiftly followed by Heeley then Owlerton Football Clubs.

Although the club was now formed, the decision of others to stay as they were left Sheffield United with no players. Advertisements were placed in the local newspapers but gleaned just three replies. It took until the end of May to recruit a squad of adequate size. Scouts headed north of the border and the first United team to kick a ball in competition was an amalgam of local amateurs and Scottish professionals. The club's very first game should have been shrouded in a little mystery given that a secret match was arranged between United and Sheffield FC at Hallam Cricket Club. However, Sheffield Wednesday captain Ted Brayshaw and a reporter followed the brake transporting United's team and were able to reveal that the fledgling club lost 3–1.

THE FIRST, IF NOT THE ONLY …

Though clubs who subsequently took United as part of their name were formed before the Blades, Sheffield United were the first to take the now well-favoured suffix. The next longest serving United – Newcastle – were founded three years later. Those pre-dating 1892 all had different incarnations until a move or incorporation of other clubs led to a change.

THE CRUCIBLE WAS A CRUCIAL VENUE

Like so many football clubs founded close to the end of the nineteenth century, a public house provided a venue for those seeking to establish a football club at Bramall Lane. The driving forces behind this plan declared their intentions at a public meeting held on 30 January 1889 at the Adelphi Hotel. The hostelry stood on the same site now used by the Crucible Theatre, which along with plays and other performances, now hosts the annual World Snooker Championships.

NO PLACE LIKE HOME

Spread over 8½ acres of land located in the south of the city, Bramall Lane derived its name from the fields on which it stood containing an approach leading to the file manufacturing business factory and private residence of David Bramall. The grounds utilised for sports were separated from other pasture by walls with a gateway leading down a dusty lane to his family estate. Work was completed in 1855 and a 90-year lease taken out at an annual rent of £70. Seven years later Bramall Lane hosted its first football match which saw Sheffield FC take on Hallam in a friendly game aimed at raising money for charity – the Lancashire Distress Fund to be precise. It is to be hoped nobody sponsored the amount of goals scored during the game. It lasted 3 hours and resulted in a goalless draw. The most remarkable result achieved at the stadium is perhaps Lockwood Brothers defeat of Nottingham Forest in an FA Cup tie during December 1886. The well regarded Forest side's 2–1 reverse is widely considered the first ever cup upset as Lockwood were ultimately a works side who only had their run ended by eventual finalists West Bromwich Albion.

United's first league game was at Bramall Lane against Lincoln City on 3 September 1892. The Blades won 4–2. Harry Hammond grabbed a hat-trick and his opening strike ensured that he became the first United player to score a Football League goal.

PIGEONS AND RABBITS ARE SAFE AT BRAMALL LANE

Sheffield United bought the ground (which the cricket club had leased from the Duke of Norfolk since 1855) following the club's 1897/98 championship-winning season. The death of the duke's loyal agent Michael Ellison that same year was a factor in the land being offered. £10,134 was the sum paid and though this may not seem much by current standards, the money was borrowed and only repaid in full half a century later. Aside from cricket, a range of other sporting endeavours have been hosted at the ground including athletics, baseball, bowls, cycling, hockey, lacrosse, tennis and rugby league. The re-formed Sheffield Eagles, who played a couple of poorly attended games at Bramall Lane in 2000 under a previous guise – Huddersfield-Sheffield Giants – commenced a tenancy in April 2010.

However, certain pastimes were banned within the land's confines and remain so. As stated in United's aims, the club was instituted to: 'promote and practice the play of cricket, football, lacrosse, lawn tennis, bowls, bicycling and tricycling, running, jumping, physical training, and the development of the human frame, and other athletic sports, games and exercises of every description, and any other game, pastime, sport, recreation, amusement or entertainment, but not pigeon shooting, rabbit coursing, or racing for money.'

There were actually moves to form an athletics club at the ground when Sheffield United were formed but that sport's governing body would not tolerate a club which employed professional sportsmen, even if those paid were not from track and field, setting up a club nor eventually staging events.

KNOCKING 'EM BANDY

Bandy is a close relation, not to say a mixture of hockey and ice hockey, in that it is played on a thin sheet of ice (though with a ball and curved sticks). Though almost exclusively practised outdoors, it also has laws very similar to Association Football. Played for over 4,000 years it was perhaps something of a good fit for a range of soccer clubs to consider, as until the latter part of the 1890s it was played on grass during summer months. Founded in 1855, Sheffield Southerand and Bandy Club were incorporated into the newly formed Sheffield United FC.

ANYONE FOR CRICKET?

Bramall Lane was one of few grounds to have had three stands rather than the four most have always boasted. The open space backed on to the cricket ground. The idea of building another stand had been mooted throughout most of the 1960s but United's return to Division One in 1971 proved the catalyst for real change. Yorkshire County Cricket Club, tenants since the ground opened, were given 2 years' notice to quit and by August 1973 the last cricket match was played. Fittingly, a Roses battle with Lancashire drew the veil on 118 years of the sport which first graced the stadium when Yorkshire entertained Sussex. League cricket had also been staged at the ground but these fixtures were moved away long before the County Championship paid its last visit.

Alongside the Oval, Bramall Lane is the only ground to have hosted both English cricket and football internationals. The summer game was limited to just one match against Australia in 1902, though. The tourists won handsomely, but more importantly it was felt receipts were insufficient and could be bettered elsewhere. Additionally industrial smog caused play to be lost in otherwise playable conditions.

GROUNDS FOR COMPLAINT

At a cost of £750,000 the new South Stand was built on the old cricket ground's outfield. The result was a full-length cantilevered stand with a seating capacity of around 8,000, which became operational in August 1975. Unfortunately, loss of the cricket revenue hit United harder than was originally expected and within 8 years the Blades, who had been able to invest little in the squad as a result of that expense, slid from the top flight to Division Four. With so much money tied up in the development of the ground, there were precious little funds available for transfers which could halt the decline. An upgrade of facilities in 1981 saw the introduction of new executive and directors' boxes, as well as dressing room facilities and a new administration department. Other developments have taken place since the early part of the twenty-first century, and, though a drive to push even more through was part of the thwarted bid to become a host stadium for 2012 Olympics and England's 2018 World Cup bid, there is no sign of ambition being stymied.

WEDNESDAY'S DAYS AT THE LANE

Wednesday Cricket Club, the forerunners of Sheffield Wednesday, also played at Bramall Lane holding a fixture in 1867 which is acclaimed as their first competitive football match. Within 12 months Wednesday won their first trophy when the Lane hosted a specially arranged tournament for clubs less than 2 years old, and they did so in the first game ever to be decided by a golden goal. The Cromwell Cup took its name from a theatre owner – Oliver Cromwell – but clearly not the one who did for Charles I. It took 10 minutes of indefinite time after the final whistle sounding for The Wednesday to beat Garrick.

The purchase of land at the Olive Grove soon after that win saw Wednesday sever their connections with a venue which first staged a game in 1862. Given that United took up residence immediately after and have not moved since, Bramall Lane is the oldest ground in the world to have continuously staged first-class football.

BACK TO THE FUTURE

Of the four stands to eventually encompass Bramall Lane, the one on John Street is perhaps the most interesting. Originally built in 1865 it remained largely untouched until 1890 when modernised with a second tier built up on certain sections. A small-scale extension was made in 1895 as the 2,000 all-seater capacity proved woefully inadequate given the sheer amount of people who wished to see United play. Receipts were so good that renowned architect Archibald Leitch, who eventually designed major parts of the Hillsborough ground, was hired to oversee the erection of a much bigger and brand new stand opened in September 1901. 3,800 seats were housed at the back of the structure with room for a further 6,000 fans just in front.

The original plans helped shape another complete rebuild when damage sustained during the Second World War necessitated it. Faithfully recreated from the old blueprints, it finally reopened in 1954 – 14 years after the damage was caused and 8 years after work began. This construction was finally demolished and totally rebuilt in 1996 at a cost of £4.2 million with a capacity of 6,500. Corners either side of the stand were filled during the summer of 2001.

A HOME FROM HOME

Bramall Lane gained redevelopment because of bomb damage which was sustained after the Luftwaffe conducted a blitz on Sheffield just before Christmas 1940. Ten bombs fell on Bramall Lane causing extensive damage to not just the John Street Stand but also the Shoreham Street Kop and Main or South Stand. The immediate reaction was to transfer all home matches to

Hillsborough and Rotherham United's Millmoor. The stadium was fit for use when the 1941/42 term kicked-off.

THE TRUE BLADES?

Sheffield Wednesday were initially known as the Blades due to the city's main industry and steel being used to make cutting implements. This nickname was one extended to most if not all Sheffield teams at one time or another, though for a while United would always be referred to as the Cutlers. This was another generic title bestowed on both the city's teams and again a steel-related nickname. That changed when Wednesday moved to Owlerton stadium in 1899 and any debate as to who should be the rightful owner of the Blades title seems to have subsided two decades later. Anecdotal evidence suggested United fans preferred to call for the Blades rather than the Cutlers. Though to further distinguish the clubs before this, Wednesday were known as the Grovites while they were playing at Olive Grove while United were referred to as the Laneites. Confusing, eh?

WHERE DID YOU GET THAT CREST?

United's emblem depicts two crossed scimitar blades and a white rose to signify the County of Yorkshire. It also includes the club's name along with the year of formation and is resplendently decorated in red, black and white – matching the club's colours. It was introduced in 1977 from which point United have been associated with the crossed blades symbol. Only a few minor alterations have been carried out since.

The design can be traced back to 1907 and the publishing of a cartoon in one of the Sheffield newspapers. An artist depicted the Owlerton-based Wednesday as an owl and United as a blade. Those early designs proved an inspiration for legendary player Jimmy Hagan who designed the emblem some 20 years before it was adopted – just prior to hanging up his boots.

Other emblems to have been used by the club include the City of Sheffield's crest. This was widely used from 1966 onwards but was also embroidered on to the players' shirts for the 1925 FA Cup final. A slightly altered version was utilised during the early part of United's history along with the club's name.

SPORTING COLOURS

United began their history in all white but had added a red stripe within a year. Blue shorts replaced the white knickerbockers players had previously worn. Over the years since, only the nature of the stripes have varied. In 1920 the lines were quite broad and accompanied by black shorts. White became the first choice short colour in 1967. Black was added to shirts in 1975. These colours remained in various jerseys worn until 1979 when United donned what was essentially a white shirt with a thick red stripe down the middle. Black and red pinstripes ran down the sides of the central stripe. Red shorts were also introduced at this time but didn't last long before replaced by the traditional black.

There was suggestion that the team wear red and white quarters during the early 1960s, although this option was not taken up after an experiment with the reserve side over Christmas 1961. There was another brief kit experiment with the introduction of a white diamond effect being laid over the stripes in 1995. However, this too only stayed for a season. Stripes can increase the potential for a clash of colours, though on one occasion it was socks that caused a problem. In a match with Coventry City the linesman asked that one of the teams change so he could distinguish them.

United have worn a variety of change strips, including the original team colours of white. Then it was white with a red V-design. White has been a fairly constant feature in away kits, while red sleeves and collars have been introduced at various times. Other colour combinations have included blue jerseys which had their first airing during the 1934/35 campaign. Orange shirts with white shorts and more latterly yellow has become a prominent colour having been mixed with a red collar and red shorts then with purple halves and matching trims. The team has also turned out in a gold strip with blue trims when colours have clashed. In order to commemorate the club's 120th anniversary, the 2009/10 season kicked off with a specially commissioned third kit – a black shirt embroidered with the names of every player to have turned out for United in the fabric.

DERRY TRIBUTE

Derry City adopted a red and white striped kit in tribute to former Blades skipper Billy Gillespie who took charge of the Irish club between 1932 and 1940. Derry had only been founded for a few years and within two seasons of the Donegal-born inside forward taking the helm, changed from a white jersey with black shorts to red and white. Though the shorts remained as they were, there was a change to a gold shirt for six years between 1956 and 1962. Otherwise the 'candystripes' have remained home colours ever since.

WHY STRIPES?
POSSIBLY SOMETHING TO SLEEP ON

Theories about the large number of clubs to have taken red
and white lines as their colours abound. But perhaps the most
interesting is that such a strip was once the cheapest to make
given that the colours were used in the making of mattresses
around the turn of the twentieth century. Any leftover cloth or
off-cuts could be picked up for relatively modest fees. Atletico
Madrid, who also play in red and white stripes, are known as *Los
Colchoneros* which – when translated from Spanish – means 'the
mattress-makers'.

Although there is insufficient evidence to be sure a cost-
minded Bramall Lane board had this in mind during the early
1890s when stripes were introduced, the manufacture of
mattresses was widespread across Yorkshire at this time, owing to
the textile industry and easy availability of other components.

NATIONAL SERVICE

Six England games have been played at Bramall Lane, the first
being against Scotland in March 1883 when the visitors won 3–2.
Scotland won the next encounter between the two a decade later,
but in April 1920 when the old enemies last met at the venue,
England secured a thrilling 5–4 victory. The Three Lions have
triumphed over every other team they have met at the home of
Sheffield United. These matches were against Ireland in February
1887 which finished 7–0; Wales who lost 4–0 on their only visit in
March 1897 and Northern Ireland who did at least manage a goal
but still found themselves on the wrong end of a 5–1 thumping
in October 1930.

NO ADMISSION

Before joining the Football League, United wanted to join the highly regarded Football Alliance but were rejected as only one team per city was allowed into membership. Sheffield Wednesday were founder members but both Manchester and Birmingham had more than a sole representative. Wednesday themselves claim they did not block any application, but United were left to lick their wounds and get on with business. They joined the Midland Counties League instead, before taking up tenure in the Northern League. Two seasons among some fine sides with high finishes proved the Blades were more than capable of holding their own should a transition to the Football League occur.

BAR ROOM GOSSIP

United board member Charles Stokes was fortunate to be spending an afternoon in the billiard room of a Southport hotel in 1891. Merseyside was an area he was hoping to exploit for talent and it is believed he was on a scouting mission, but after eavesdropping on a conversation he learned that Preston North End were about to allow some of a team known as 'The Invincibles' to leave Deepdale. He moved swiftly and met counterparts at the Lancashire club agreeing fees to purchase three of the most important players United would call on over the Victorian era – centre-half Billy Hendry (who became captain), outside left Jack Drummond and inside forward Sammy Dobson. This trio added to the talent already in place and helped the club enjoy much success during the decade which followed. Starting with a promotion to Division One, they ended with silverware as champions, then FA Cup holders.

HIGHS AND LOWS

Matches with other Yorkshire clubs understandably make for interesting clashes, and have created record attendances at Bramall Lane. Regardless of hail, rain or sun, huge numbers make their way to the ground for these encounters. Even extreme cold fails to put hardy souls from both sides off. The highest number paying to watch a game was 68,287 for an FA Cup encounter with Leeds United in February 1936. The club's Football League record was set by the 59,555 fans packing the ground to see a Sheffield derby played during January 1927. Away from the Lane, a meeting with Wednesday at Hillsborough set a high-point for the third tier of English football – 49,309 spectators took in a match on Boxing Day 1979.

Although exact figures are hard to determine due to the scant nature of early record-keeping, United's lowest verified attendance in the Football League is 4,014 for the visit of Nottingham Forest in 1934/35. That said, observers estimated that there were approximately 2,500 at the United v Millwall game in 1894/95, which if true, would constitute the club's lowest crowd ever to attend at game at Bramall Lane. Post-war figures show the worst figure to be a slightly healthier 6,647 for the game against Crystal Palace in 1986/87. It is estimated that just 500 fans turned up to see a clash with Darwen in 1892/93.

The biggest crowd ever to watch a game involving the Blades is 114,815. That number turned up at Crystal Palace to watch the first game of the 1901 FA Cup final against Tottenham Hotspur.

ZULUS

In 1879 Sheffield was the very centre of world football. There were as many soccer teams in Sheffield at the time as there were steel factories. But, far away from the hallowed fields of England, war raged against the Zulus in South Africa. The British Army eventually repelled their enemy but at a very high cost in terms of both money and soldiers.

In a somewhat bizarre attempt to raise funds for the widows and orphans of the Boer War, a team was created of white players, which adopted the title Zulus. Greats of the game, such as Scotsman Jack Hunter, named themselves after some of the kings and chiefs of the Zulu tribes taking on the Blades at Bramall Lane. They blackened their faces and hands with burnt corks, wore black jerseys and covered their legs in full-length stockings before finishing the effect with feathered head-dress and white beads around their necks. They claimed a 5–4 victory and, buoyed by their success, toured their team around the country never losing a game. There was also an offer to tour South Africa.

Placing the attitudes of modern society and what is found acceptable with regard to race to one side, there was controversy about the Zulu team which set out to play a host of additional games over the next three years. However, once it was discovered that personal gain for the players rather than good causes was the aim, a scandal brewed. Receiving money for playing was an illegal practice at the time and they were disbanded.

PENALTY!

Jack Scott was the man entrusted with the club's first penalty during a Northern League game with Middlesbrough in October 1891. However, just moments later he became the first United player to miss a spot-kick. Fortunately the blunder had no bearing on the game which United still won 2–1. Ernest Needham was the first successful penalty-taker in March 1894 against Blackburn Rovers. The strike proved to be the decisive goal in a 3–2 win. Not to say that Needham had it all his own way 12 yards out. He earned himself an unfortunate place in the record books when becoming the first player to score and miss a penalty in the same game five years later.

Strictly speaking, Jack Scott's penalty was not the first drama involving a spot-kick. The rule had been brought in for the 1891/92 season. In the initial game of that Northern League campaign, Sunderland Albion were the opposition. United recorded a 4–3 win with one of the opposing goals coming from a penalty. However, the kick was disallowed after the game finished when the referee, a little troubled by his new responsibilities, felt doubts about his earlier decision creeping in. After a consultation with the rule book, the goal was rescinded and the result officially declared as a 4–2 for United.

Colin Morris is the Blades' most prolific scorer from the spot with 35 successful conversions. Morris also holds the record for the most penalties missed with 12. Outside those who netted the odd penalty they took, the best goals to penalties taken ratio must go to Fred Furniss who missed just one of his 17 attempts – in a 7–3 win over Wednesday in September 1951.

A MAN DOWN FROM THE START

United began a league game against West Bromwich Albion in April 1898 with just 10 men. Although the numbers were evened during the early part of the game that disadvantage didn't hamper the Blades who won 2–0.

TAKING A BATTERING FROM THE ELEMENTS

The British climate has taken its toll on various games. On 12 November 1894 wind and rain battered Villa Park so hard that 4 United players were forced to leave the field at one point. In October 1932 the Blades finished a game against Blackburn Rovers with 8 men after 3 needed treatment for exposure as again wind, sleet and rain took its toll on the players. Rovers took full advantage of the superior numbers coasting to a 3–0 win, though they also played without a couple of players at stages and the referee had to go off after collapsing. One of his linesmen was forced to take over in his absence. On 15 January 1938 in a game with Newcastle United the players were withdrawn from the field for 5 minutes due to a torrential downpour. They were allowed to finish the match which the Blades won 4–0. Twenty-four years earlier a league game between the two clubs saw the injury depleted Magpies start with 8 players.

Adverse weather is not the only extreme players are expected to toil in. For the opening fixture of the 1906/07 season against Derby County on 1 September, the temperature in the shade was an incredible 90°F. Despite the intense heat, United finished on top with a 2–0 win.

DANGER UXB!

Perhaps the most unusual reason a match has been postponed from its scheduled date was the occasion a league game with Oldham Athletic was delayed courtesy of an unexploded Second World War bomb being found near to the ground. Due to take place on 7 February 1993, the fixture took place the following Tuesday with the Blades winning 2–0.

LATE KICK-OFF

Matches can be delayed for a multitude of reasons: some serious, some trivial. Some last longer than others but perhaps the most interesting was a 5-minute wait United and Barnsley players had at Bramall Lane in February 1959 while a dog chased one of the practice balls. It possibly affected the visiting players more as the Blades won comfortably 5–0.

AN UNASSUMING LEGEND

Jimmy Hagan came to Bramall Lane as a 20-year-old recruit from Derby County in 1938. He made an impressive start to his United career by scoring a hat-trick in the game against Spurs which ensured the club's promotion back to Division One towards the end of that first campaign. The intervention of the Second World War just months later probably took the best years of his career and robbed him of going down in history as one of the greatest players the Football League has ever seen. Those lucky enough to witness him in full flow would probably say he was the most skilful and creative midfield man on view. At home on either side of the field he could also hit a ball off either foot with equal strength. His excellent ball–control on his left or right peg (even in the most difficult conditions) and his ability to trick his opponents also created many chances for others. An otherwise perfect disciplinary record was slightly tarnished by a sending-off against Swansea Town in December 1952. United had the game won, especially after Hagan had scored the last of 7 goals. However, he became involved in a fracas with Swansea's Lucas just in front of the John Street Stand. There was said to be a history of antagonism between the two players, yet very few people saw the incident which led to the flare-up.

The only people who could not see his qualities were the England selectors. Hagan made a number of wartime international teamsheets, but was generally considered too free-wheeling to be a part of their plans. The postwar clamour for him to be reinstated to the international fray encompassed far more than just the United fans and became something of a nationwide campaign.

However, Hagan was selected for England duty just once in 1948 when he lined up with the likes of Stanley Matthews, Tommy Lawton and Len Shackleton in a forward-thinking side which could only manage a 0–0 in Denmark. Blackpool's Stan Mortensen returned when the national side next played a fortnight later in Belfast.

There was talk of him signing for Sheffield Wednesday in 1951 and although a huge fee of £32,500 – a British record – was agreed between the two clubs, Hagan just couldn't make the switch. He stayed and claimed a Second Division championship-winners medal in 1953. Four years later he played his final league game for the Blades in September, ironically enough at the Baseball Ground where it all began for him two decades earlier. After retiring he went on to manage extensively in Portugal. With Benfica he won 3 Portuguese championships in a row plus their equivalent of the FA Cup. He also guided the side to the semi-finals of the European Cup. Eusébio was an important member of that side and the two enjoyed a mutual respect and great friendship. However, failure to see eye-to-eye over Eusébio's testimonial cost Hagan his job at the Estádio da Luz. Later he managed Benfica's rivals Sporting Lisbon. Sadly Jimmy passed away in 1998.

KICKING OFF A WHOLE NEW BALL GAME

On 15 August 1992, the Premiership's debut day, Brian Deane went down in history as the scorer of the new division's first goal. On a warm Yorkshire afternoon the striker notched the first in a 2–1 win over eventual champions Manchester United. Chelsea's Mick Harford and Paul Williams of Coventry City struck 4 minutes later in their respective games.

THE REFEREE HAS GIVEN ANOTHER CORNER

It is commonly believed that United hold the record for the most corner kicks won during a game – 28 were taken on 14 October 1989 in the home match with West Ham United, who had just one awarded but still ran out 2–0 winners.

BOTH SIDES OF THE CITY

Thirty-three players have played for the Blades as well as the Owls either as fully-fledged signings or as part of loan deals for one or other of the city's clubs. Alan Quinn is the only player to score for both clubs in derby games and the most recent to make a switch directly between the clubs, in the summer of 2004.

Carl Bradshaw	Derek Geary	Brian Marwood	Neil Ramsbottom
Leigh Bromby	James Harrop	Jon-Paul McGovern	Walter Rickett
Franz Carr	Jack Hudson	Billy Mellors	Wilf Rostron
Joe Cockroft	David Johnson	Billy Mosforth	Bernard Shaw
Terry Curran	Tommy Johnson	Bernard Oxley	Simon Stainrod
David Ford	Jeff King	Alan Quinn	Charles Taylor
Oliver Tummon	Imre Varadi	George Walker	Alan Warboys
Dean Windass	Earl Barrett	Owen Morrison	Walter Rickett
Carl Robinson			

George Hunt, a prolific scorer who saw his career out at Wednesday, never played in a first-team game for the Blades but was offered a trial. Surprisingly United decided not to follow their interest up despite the forward netting 4 goals during the game they arranged. Jack Smith was an amateur at Hillsborough before joining United and playing almost 400 games.

Though not directly traded between both clubs, just 6 days after turning out for the Blades Earl Barrett was making his Owls debut. The England international had spent 5 weeks on loan at United from Everton during the 1997/98 season, gaining first-team football during an injury-plagued few years. Courtesy of his contribution to United the defender was offered terms by Sheffield Wednesday who had watched his progress. So effectively, 48 hours after officially leaving Bramall Lane, he was being photographed at Hillsborough on completing a free transfer. Sadly more fitness setbacks ended his career in 2000. Derek Geary sandwiched 3 months at Stockport County between his time at Hillsborough and signing in at Bramall Lane.

Walter Rickett started his career with Sheffield United. He actually scored on his debut and in the process became one of the few players to have done so with his first touch. In a strange twist of fate the opposition that day were Wednesday. He atoned for that perceived sin by Owls fans when he signed on at Hillsborough in October 1949 and helped the club claim two Second Division championships during the early 1950s.

For some, turning out for both Wednesday and United proved nothing more than artistic license. Mel Sterland and Charlie Williamson's defections to the Blades was fictional. Both played Sheffield United players in the film *When Saturday Comes*. Each served a few clubs after leaving Wednesday, but United were not among them. Not only players have found themselves straddling both sides of the divide. Charles Stokes was an original member of the Wednesday committee but subsequently became a founder member of Sheffield United. Derek Dooley played for and managed the Owls then served the Blades as a commercial manager (among other roles) before becoming managing director then chairman of United's Football Club board.

THE ULTIMATE FOOTBALL MERCENARY?

There is constant criticism and debate about mercenary attitudes of players within the modern game but even a player like Nicolas Anelka or Fabrizio Ravanelli would have struggled to keep up with the record of Willie Mosforth. In the 1870s, when the man better known as Billy played, no strict contracts existed which left him free to play for whichever club took his fancy. Quite often this would include a couple at the same time and on more than one occasion he turned out for both Wednesday and Sheffield Albion on the same day. Only when the two met did he have to make a choice. Such was his ability that when Wednesday were due to face Albion, Owls' fans offered him cash to change sides. The offer was readily taken up and moments before kick-off he swapped allegiances. Wednesday tied him down in 1877 but in the best traditions of the early part of his career he left in 1889 to join United. Bramall Lane was his last club. He also served Sheffield Rovers, Hallam and Sheffield Zulus.

AN OWL WHO FEATHERED THE NEST

Although he was one of Sheffield Wednesday's most celebrated players (with over 400 appearances under his belt), Teddy Davison had no hesitation in accepting the manager/secretary's post at Bramall Lane once it was offered to him. Just two seasons after his appointment the Blades were relegated, but narrowly missed out on promotion in 1936 and 1938. Only 12 months after that last near miss, United did make the top flight and to make the glory even sweeter it came at the expense of Davison's old team. Unfortunately the war against Hitler disrupted the first season back in the big-time. The seeming mediocrity of Davison's early years in charge doesn't tell the whole story. United reached the 1936 FA Cup final and developed a youth policy almost second to none in the entire Football League. His guiding principles almost reaped rich dividends after the war when United mounted a concerted effort in both the league and cup. Open cheque books disrupted the progress made and poorer quality replacements led to another relegation in 1949. Despite pulling his side back onto something of an even keel during the early 1950s, Davison decided to retire in the summer of 1952.

Ian Porterfield is another former Owl to have taken charge of team affairs at Bramall Lane. He spent 3 years at Hillsborough from 1977 and within 12 months of leaving was starting the tough job of rebuilding the Blades' shattered ambitions. This he duly did, leading them from the Fourth to Second Divisions in just 3 seasons before being sacked. Former Wednesday captain Jack Hudson is another to have joined the coaching staff at Bramall Lane. So too George Waller, who joined United in 1892 and was pressed into action a few times.

A LEPPARD PREPARED TO CHANGE HIS STRIPES?

Though a boyhood Wednesday fan and a regular at Hillsborough, Def Leppard's Rob Savage only turned to music after deciding not to pursue a football career. Instead of looking for another club, he formed a band called Atomic Mass a year after leaving the Blades in 1977. This eventually became the multi-million selling group he has remained a member of for almost three and a half decades.

DERBY DAYS

The Sheffield derby may not be the most high-profile but remains one of the most fiercely contested rivalries in European soccer. It is even said that Wednesdayites refrain from eating bacon on matchday mornings due to its red and white colours. Strictly speaking, it is the oldest too. But the first competitive encounter between clubs from the city wasn't between United and Wednesday. It was an FA Cup tie between Sheffield FC and Sheffield Providence in 1879. The Blades and Owls only met for the first time 11 years later. From the 125 games played since both teams entered the Football League, Sheffield United hold the whip hand with 4 victories more than Wednesday have recorded. The actual figues are 45 to 41 with 39 games drawn.

The two giants got to pit their wits against each other for the first time on 15 December 1890 in a friendly. Despite the match being played on a Monday afternoon just over a week before Christmas, 10,000 fans ventured out to the Olive Grove. Overhead the sky was as grey as Wednesday's recent form. The home club were bottom of the Football Alliance and had been forced to suffer the ultimate indignity of watching their neighbours establish themselves firmly in their league – albeit a different one. To add further insult to injury the recently formed visitors took the lead through Robertson after 20 minutes, though an equaliser was found by the end. A return fixture at Bramall Lane a few weeks later proved just as pulsating as the first encounter. This time it was Wednesday's turn to draw first blood and when the advantage was stretched to 2–0 it seemed the visitors would brighten an otherwise damp squib of a season by claiming an historic double. United had other ideas and claimed a remarkable 3–2 victory. Some of the bad blood during these early years could be put down to the defection of a number of players from Wednesday to United when the Blades were formed.

United's best win against Wednesday is a 7–3 thrashing on 8 September 1951. On the flip side the club's worst defeat came when both teams were at a low ebb. Each languished in the Third Division when Wednesday recorded a 4–0 home win on Boxing Day 1979.

Only one derby match has taken place outside the city: at Wembley in the FA Cup semi-final played on 3 April 1993. The Owls were victorious thanks to Mark Bright and Chris Waddle's goals cancelling out Alan Cork's strike, and they went on to play Arsenal in the final.

KNIVES OFTEN OUT IN THE STEEL CITY

Rivalry between the Sheffield clubs has been intensified by a number of high-profile games and the fact that on many occasions both have been chasing the same prize. At the end of the 1938/39 season the Owls and the Blades vied for the final escape pod back into Division One. United lay 1 point behind Wednesday but needed to beat Spurs to pip their neighbours at the finishing line. A draw would not be enough, owing to Wednesday's superior goal difference. The Owls had completed their programme a week earlier beating Spurs who were powerless to resist the Blades and received a 6–1 hammering.

To level matters United missed out by just 0.008 of a goal when Tottenham again, who were runaway champions of the second tier, earned a 0–0 draw with Wednesday on the final day of the 1949/50 season. The Owls then leapfrogged the Blades. A 1–1 draw would have put each of the Sheffield clubs level on not just points but goal average. Under competition rules a one-off match would have decided the runners-up spot.

Bad blood was never more evident than in an FA Cup game a decade later. In fact it was on show almost all over the pitch. The tie was played at Owlerton and was so bad-tempered that through a combination of injury and sendings-off, United finished with 9 men and Wednesday with 8. Most of the players who did make it through the entire game limped off the field. United as cup holders and leaders of the First Division were clear favourites to go through, despite the Owls being in similar form and topping Division Two.

BATTING ABOVE THEIR AVERAGE

By far the most intriguing set of derby games took place at the end of the 1930s when United and Wednesday players clashed in a series of cricket matches at Bramall Lane. Given both clubs' historical roots it seems a rather fitting challenge.

STANIFORTH'S FLAG DAY

Officials are seldom appreciated and often much maligned, incurring the wrath of many football supporters including Blades fans. However, those present for a Division One game at Stamford Bridge on 10 February 1973 were forced to hold their tongues when United's Paul Staniforth ran the line during the game. Initially named as the Blades' substitute, he became a temporary replacement when the designated linesman was incapacitated. United drew no advantage from having a man among the officials' camp as Chelsea ran out 4–2 winners on the day.

Linesman Edward Martin was knocked unconscious by a Sheffield United fan in January 1998, irate at the dismissal of goalkeeper Simon Tracey after a collision with Portsmouth midfielder Sammy Igoe during first-half injury time. The decision was made by referee Mark Halsey on advice from the Somerset official who collapsed as defender Sean Derry donned the goalkeeper jersey. Eye-witnesses saw Mr Martin go to ground after being punched. A 3-month sentence was handed down to the fan along with a lifelong ban from Bramall Lane.

THE WAR YEARS

Despite the First World War starting in 1914 it took the best part of 2 years for the powers that be to suspend play within the Football League. Teams kept playing, but in specially organised contests against teams geographically nearby. From September 1915 to April 1919 United took part in the Section (Principal Tournament). The Midland Section (Subsidiary Tournament) was introduced for the last half-dozen games of the campaign. United won the Midland Subsidiary Tournament in 1919.

The advent of the Second World War was a totally different matter. The possible repercussions of an all-out conflict with Hitler's Germany were plain for all to see. It meant that the 1939/40 league campaign was just 3 games old when abandoned. Regional divisions were set up once more, but unlike those established during the previous hostilities, allowed many changes to personnel ensuring Ministry of Defence guidelines on travel, crowding and air raids were satisfied. United joined the Football League North. In as much as these things matter, the Blades achieved a modicum of success winning the championship in 1946 and in the process becoming the first club to win any form of championship after conceding 5 goals or more in the opening game of the season. The record was only paralleled by Norwich City in 2009/10. Newcastle United seemed to have highlighted enough weaknesses in the Blades side that would consign them to a moderate season when they lost 6–0. However, a prodigious run of form saw the team lose just another 8 matches after that game.

The peculiar circumstances of both world wars saw Wednesday and United share many players. Quite often during the same season in the First World War. These included Harold Bell, Ernest Blackwell, H. Booth, Charles Brelsford, Harold Buddery, Tom Cawley, S. Ford, Joseph Godfrey, Percy Oldacre, A. Price, Harold Salt, H. Spratt and Oliver Tummon.

Slightly fewer were able to make the same kind of switches during the next conflict, with only Harold Barton, Alf Calverley, Bob Curry, Ken Gadsbury, Tom Johnson, George Laking, Walter Millership, Jack Smith, Hugh Swift and Fred White wearing the shirts of both sides.

RESERVING JUDGEMENT

Until 1891 there was no formal reserve side fielded by United and for the first 3 years of their existence the county FA insisted the side below first-team level be known as the Sheffield Strollers and play in the Hallamshire League which they won at the first attempt. A name change to Sheffield United Reserves brought a little more luck and within the next 4 seasons the second string had claimed the Sheffield Association League and the Wharncliffe Charity Cup in 1897. The championship of the West Yorkshire League was secured the following term.

In 1898 there was another change of league as along with many other senior clubs in the region, the reserves joined the Midland League. An electric pace was set as the second XI claimed 4 of the first 8 titles they were able to compete for. Those winning seasons were the 1900/01, 1903/04, 1904/05 and 1906/07 campaigns. The Wharncliffe Cup was won again in 1904. In 1921 United opted to join the Central League which was born following the merger of the Midland League with its Northern counterpart.

The reserves showed the new competition was to their liking as they took the championship at their first attempt. Success has been in relatively short supply since that time. There was a sole title in 1966 but nothing else until the 2002/03 campaign, though the Pontin's League Cup was claimed in 1998.

CUBAN DEALS

Canadian youth international Ryan Gyaki was touring Cuba with Calgary Storm when spotted by United scouts as a 16-year-old and invited to join the Bramall Lane youth set-up. After steady progress and starring at the FIFA World Youth Championship in 2005 he graduated to the reserves later in the same year but on his debut ruptured knee ligaments and was forced to sit out a whole season. After recuperating he found it impossible to make much of a mark and joined Hansa Rostock II.

WHAT A GOAL, WHAT A CELEBRATION!

Goal celebrations are often as well practised and drilled on the training pitch as any free-kick or other set-piece routine. One of the most noted salutes to a rippling net of recent times is Peter Beagrie's somersault. A trademark often copied since, but certainly one the winger pioneered – at least on the domestic scene. Over a career which lasted more than two decades, the back flips got fewer as age got the better of his agility and the risk of injury from the party trick increased. Chronic tendonitis in his left patella was another huge hindrance. As his time at Bramall Lane encompassed his early twenties, most of his 11 goals for the Blades (many of them superb strikes after runs down the flank), were marked in that acrobatic manner. They were also just as crowd-pleasing as the twists and turns which took him past many hapless defenders. There were also cartwheels in the boardroom as a £35,000 acquisition from the financially stricken Middlesbrough realised almost a threefold profit when Stoke City came in with a £210,000 bid during the summer of 1988.

VILLAINS OF THE PEACE

Of the teams United have faced most often, their worst record is against Aston Villa. Over the course of 128 league and cup games the two clubs have contested, Villa have won 61 with United claiming only 37 victories – 30 have ended in draws. The Blades last tasted victory in December 1991 and the worst defeat was a 6–1 thrashing at Villa Park in February 1904, although United had inflicted a 6–0 hammering on Villa two years earlier.

WHAT A START!

The Blades' best-ever start to a season is the 22 games they went unbeaten at the beginning of the 1899/1900 campaign. In 1971 United went another 22 games undefeated, split over two seasons from March to October. In the process of building that run – 15 wins and 7 draws – the Blades achieved promotion back to the top flight and set a blistering pace on their return to Division One before Manchester United inflicted a first defeat of the new campaign.

A FOOTBALLING PIONEER

Although he made just one league appearance for United – a consequence of being William Foulke's understudy – goalkeeper Arthur Wharton is something of a *cause célèbre* among British footballers due to the fact he was the first black professional player to grace the English game.

He was born in Africa on The Gold Coast, the country now known as Ghana, in 1865 to mixed-race parents. His father was half-Grenadian and half-Scottish, his mother half-Scottish and half-Fante (the royal family of Ekumfie). In less diverse times than the present day, Wharton started his career at 19, turning out for Darlington, Preston North End, Rotherham, Sheffield United, Stalybridge Rovers, Ashton North End and Stockport County.

Wharton was a naturally acrobatic man who would bound around his area with ease and often use his posts to gain purchase. He was also a fleet-footed player with pace who was often fancied to outshine any winger – something he proved more than capable of on the few occasions he took to the flank in order to get a game and when he raced out to deny strikers the ball. Such was his athletic prowess that he was at one stage an Amateur Athletics Association 100 yards champion. The run which won him that accolade at Stamford Bridge came at the age of 21 and saw him become the first man to run the distance in 10 seconds at a national championship. His time was officially adopted as a world record. He was also a professional cricketer who played for a number of sides but died aged 65 in 1930 after many years spent as a miner working in the Yorkshire coalfields. Unfortunately he passed away in near poverty, an alcoholic who had fathered many illegitimate children. Even with an extensive lineage his family were unable to afford so much as a gravestone for his burial place in Edlington near Doncaster. The site lay unmarked until 1997 when more than £1,000 was raised to erect a headstone.

THEY THINK IT'S ALL OVER

In the third round of the 1998/99 FA Cup, United faced fellow Division One side Notts County. The team was enduring an indifferent run of form and looked set to continue their misery when trailing 3–1 with 5 minutes to go. That was until a remarkable turn of fortune. Vas Borbokis had scored just before half-time. United levelled with goals from David Holdsworth and Marcelo. The Portuguese scored with almost the last kick of normal time and 4 minutes into the extra period he went on to claim a winner.

BLADES IN THE PREMIERSHIP

Over 3 Premiership campaigns the Blades have grabbed a couple of competition records. Unfortunately none are of the type most clubs would wish to hold. They are:

Most draws in a season	18	jointly held with Manchester City and Southampton
Fewest away goals in a season	8	jointly held with Middlesbrough and Southampton

SONGS TO SING

United fans have always had a wide repertoire of songs and chants suitable for most occasions. Among the favourites on the jukebox is 'The Greasy Chip Butty Song', as sung to the tune of John Denver hit 'Annie's Song'.

> You fill up my senses
> Like a gallon of Magnet
> Like a packet of Woodbines
> Like a good pinch of snuff
> Like a night out in Sheffield
> Like a greasy chip butty
> Oh Sheffield United
> Come thrill me again . . .
> Na na na na naa naa naaaaa, ooo!

After Sheffield United took over the Chengdu Wuniu the *Sheffield Star* newspaper penned a Chinese alternative:

> You fill up my senses
> Like a gallon of soy sauce
> Like a packet of chopsticks
> Like a good crispy duck
> Like a night out in Chengdu
> Like a greasy egg noodle
> Like Chengdu 'n' United
> Come thrill me again . . .

COUNTY CHAMPIONS

Although United withdrew from the County Cup in 1981 they have won the trophy on 21 occasions. The trophy was shared with Sheffield Wednesday in 1939 and Barnsley in 1971. A win by the reserves in 1964 is also included. The initial victory was the first time the trophy was up for grabs and the last win came from the final season in which the Blades contested the trophy.

HITTING THE DOUBLES

Cardiff City's 11–2 defeat in Division One on New Year's Day 1926 is the best win ever witnessed by a Bramall Lane crowd. The Blades had scored a 10–0 victory at Burslem Port Vale not long after formation. The third and last time United hit double figures was back in January 1929 when Burnley were thrashed by the same scoreline. Just a week earlier the Clarets had won an FA Cup tie between the pair.

UNLUCKY NUMBERS

Sheffield United have been involved in some entertaining but ultimately fruitless encounters in terms of points. On three occasions the opposition have scored 7 at Bramall Lane. Huddersfield Town recorded a 7–1 win in November 1927 – which stands as the highest margin for a home defeat. Blackburn Rovers gained the better of a dozen goals in a 7–5 victory in March 1930. Another Yorkshire derby brought Rotherham United a 7–2 win in December 1956.

The highest aggregate score in both league and cup defeats is 13 – certainly an unlucky number for the Blades given a 10–3 win by Middlesbrough at Ayresome Park and the 13–0 hammering inflicted by Bolton Wanderers in the 1889/90 FA Cup. The Trotters cruised to that still-standing competition record win at Burnden Park.

The Blades' biggest home defeat in the cup is a 9–1 hammering in 1890/91. The biggest margin of defeat on the road is also 8 goals. This came when United travelled to Middlesbrough during the 1933/34 league season and came home on the receiving end of a 10–2 hammering.

The Blades have fallen victim to defeat by 7 clear goals on occasion. This was the gap twice for Arsenal who won 8–1 in April 1930 and 9–2 on Christmas Eve 1932. To complete the misery inflicted by North London sides, Tottenham Hotspur posted 7 without reply at White Hart Lane in November 1949.

UNITED! UNITED! UNITED! UNITED! UNITED! UNITED! UNITED!

Imre Varadi was often termed something of a journeyman footballer, and with employment by 16 clubs there is more than a grain of truth in that. The Blades were his first league club and though he played just a handful of games and went on to be something of a Sheffield Wednesday legend throughout his career, he was a 'United' man. On leaving Bramall Lane he played for another 6 clubs with that suffix added to their names: Newcastle, Leeds, Oxford, Rotherham, Boston and Scunthorpe. Despite playing for both Sheffield outfits, Varadi never featured in a Steel City derby.

SEASON'S BEST

The prolific Harry Johnson scored over 200 goals during his time at Bramall Lane. His season's best was a more than creditable 33 in 1927/28 but even he has to doff his cap to Jimmy Dunne, who scored the most in a single term for Sheffield United. Recording 41 during the 1930/31 campaign he broke his own record of 36 set a season earlier. His tally for the season was brought up to a half-century courtesy of cup goals. It is a benchmark that still stands over 70 years later. Though he failed to reach the same target by the close of the 1931/32 term, Dunne did go on something of a scoring burst notching at least once in 12 consecutive games. In total he amassed 19 during that run. Part of the reason for his prolific scoring was an amazing ability with not only his feet but his head, too. He was seen as one of the outstanding forwards of his day when the ball was in the air, and scored many of his 167 goals for the club in aerial combat.

In terms of sustained scoring Brian Deane hit 2 hat-tricks within 4 days. The first was in a third round FA Cup replay win over Burnley and the second a Premier League clash with Ipswich Town. Jimmy Dunne had gone slightly better 63 years earlier when he scored 4 goals twice in games against West Ham United and Leicester City within the space of 3 days

GOALSCORING FEATS

Harry Hammond and Harry Johnson hold the record for scoring the most goals in a single league game with 5. Both were recorded on a Boxing Day. Hammond's feat was against Bootle in 1892 and Johnson's in 1927 versus West Ham United. Christmas Eve is the least appealing day of the festive season for the Blades who conceded the largest tally against by a single player – the 5 Jack Lambert scored in a 9–2 reverse at Highbury in 1932.

Arthur Brown scored 6 in a friendly game with Gainsborough Town while Jimmy Dunne, Jack Scott and Adrian Littlejohn have all grabbed a nap-hand in friendlies. In wartime games Fred Stone also scored 5 when United met Mansfield Town in 1942. In pre-Football League times Scott put five past Burnley in 1892.

DUNNE'S DOZEN

Consecutive scoring feats have been set by Jimmy Dunne who scored at least once in 12 successive games during the 1931/32 season. Arthur Brown scored for 8 games running over the course of the 1906/07 campaign. A feat equalled by Keith Edwards 70 years later.

TOP OF THE CHARTS

Harry Johnson Jnr is the club's leading goalscorer. His 205 league strikes came from just over 300 games between 1919 and 1930. Johnson is also the top scorer in the FA Cup with 20. Jimmy Dunne's ratio of 167 goals from 190 league games over 8 Division One seasons is a mark few players have troubled during the intervening years and despite the modern-day Football League having far bigger divisions and consequently more games it seems to be in no immediate danger of being overhauled.

DEREK SETS THE PACE

Derek Pace was a United legend and as a centre forward could have done no more than score on his debut then follow that up with another strike in his first Sheffield derby. By the time he left Bramall Lane in 1964, he had scored 175 goals from 302 appearances by virtue of his sheer ability to send an unstoppable effort in on goal with any part of his body. A fast player, he was also quick off the mark and unbeatable over sprints and short distances – which bought him space to exploit even in tight areas. The club's top scorer over each of his 6 seasons, his nickname 'Doc' came as a result of his 2-year National Service call-up (he served in the Medical Corps).

LONG SERVICE

Joe Shaw is the only player to have made over 600 appearances in the league which, when combined with his 51 FA Cup outings, make up a huge chunk of his 690 aggregate games for the club. Both the league and FA Cup figures are competition records for the Blades, although Alan Hodgkinson finished just 1 game short of equalling the tally in the cup. Alan Woodward sets the mark in the League Cup with 30 appearances plus 2 outings from the bench. These 3 players are the leading appearance makers in the Football League. Joe Shaw leads the way with 631 outings. Hodgkinson played 576 games and Alan Woodward started 536 matches and was introduced from the bench twice.

HOMESICK BLUES

Inside forward Cameron Evans, better known in his native Scotland as Cammie, found his chances at Rangers restricted. Without a first-team appearance he was grateful for the chance to prove his worth at Bramall Lane when an offer came in the final days of November 1968. His stay didn't extend to any point in December. He spent 48 hours as a Sheffield United player, which took in a Central League game, before deciding he wanted a return to Scotland. He headed back across Hadrian's Wall and joined Kilmarnock. Less than a year later he moved on joining Queen of the South and then Stranraer. His professional career ended in 1973.

Homesickness assisted the Blades in landing one of the club's legends, Keith Edwards, who after joining Leyton Orient as a teenager in order to please his father (a lifelong 'Os' fan), took the chance to move back towards his Teesside birthplace and accepted terms from Sheffield United.

SHOTGUN DEBUTS

One player who did not expect to guest for the Blades during a wartime match was L. Butcher, who was called up when United reported to Preston North End's Deepdale ground a player short. A message went out to the nearby Fulwood Garrison in order to land a volunteer.

Harry Johnson Jnr. was keen to make his way from steelworks to football field and emulate his father in turning out for the Blades. But he may have been forgiven if he had second thoughts after his debut in a reserve match at Heckmondwike. A 'Hecky' fan pointed a gun at him. To much relief the weapon wasn't loaded.

MAKING A SPECTACLE
OF THE OPPOSITION

The Blades' first-ever FA Cup game set a mark for the club's best-ever win in the competition. Scarborough were the opponents for a 6–1 thrashing in September 1889. Loughborough also suffered at the hands of United when that best-ever score was equalled the following year. The Blades 10–0 hammering of Burslem Port Vale on 10 December 1892 is not only United's record league win, it also remains the heaviest ever win any league team has inflicted away from home. It is also the only occasion a visiting side has reached double figures. Some of the damage was blamed on the Burslem keeper losing his spectacles in the mud and snow.

GOALKEEPERS ARE DIFFERENT

Rab Hewlett, a renowned keeper from Sheffield United's past and signed from Gainsborough Trinity, was one of a select band of goalkeepers to have played in spectacles. Another sartorial distinction for a keeper was Joe Lievesley becoming the first stopper to turn out in a jersey different from the rest of his colleagues in 1909, following a dictat from the FA.

MINOR HONOURS

Possibly the most diverse tournament the Blades have ever participated in came at the close of the 1971/72 campaign. United were invited to take on Zambian club side Rokana and a national XI. By virtue of 3 wins plus a draw, the trophy was claimed. Tom McAlister proved to be the hero in the final game saving two penalty kicks.

Other games to have been decided on penalties include games in the Gibraltar International Tournament and the Pennine Radio Cup.

CHEEKY GOALS

From long-distance screamers to lucky deflections, Sheffield United players have scored every type of goal, but perhaps the cheekiest was netted by Dean Saunders against Port Vale in March 1998. Then a wily old-pro nearing his 34th birthday with time in the English, Turkish and Portuguese top flights plus more than 50 caps under his belt, he raced goalkeeper Paul Musselwhite for a ball towards the touchline in the final minute of normal time.

Still in his twenties, the keeper was always likely to win but lacked the Welshman's guile. Merely touching the ball out for a throw in was a mistake on Musselwhite's behalf, as reinforcements were some distance away. The ball couldn't just be thrown into the net and Saunders was not allowed to drop it on his own feet. But throwing it against the keeper's back allowed him to take a shot then curl a 25-yard effort around the retreating (not to mention red-faced) goalie. As Wayne Corden pulled one back during injury time it was an important strike which brought 3 vital points towards a nail biting play-off qualification – achieved on goal difference.

A LOVELY SUM

A princely £261,758 was collected in gate receipts when the Blades hosted Manchester United in the 5th round of the FA Cup on Valentine's Day 1993. It remained by far the largest pay day in the club's history until £467,036 was raised through the turnstiles for a First Division play-off semi-final with Nottingham Forest on 15 May 2003. The game was well worth the entrance fee. United went through after a 4–3 extra-time win. 3 goals were scored during the additional period, 2 of which were players from each side putting through their own nets.

MARATHON RUNNING

United featured in the first of 2 FA Cup semi-finals to have been contested over 4 games – although it is worth pointing out that one of those matches – the third – was abandoned. Liverpool were the opponents back in 1899 with Nottingham playing host to the first match which finished all square at 2–2. Hedley opened the scoring and Walter Bennett grabbed an equaliser. The next game, played at Burnden Park, looked like it was going to the Merseysiders who led 4–2 when Jack Cox scored after 72 minutes, but Fred Priest grabbed a late brace to level affairs by the final whistle. A ground in Fallowfield, Manchester, staged the next contest. Only 45 minutes of play was possible owing to the packed crowd spilling onto the field. Liverpool led 1–0 when the game was eventually abandoned at 6 p.m. – 2½ hours after kick-off. Injuries to 4 regulars (including the highly influential Bill Foulke) seemed to give Liverpool the edge for the rescheduled tie which took place 3 days later. Derby County's Baseball Ground comfortably accommodated the paying public who witnessed United win through to the final.

MODELS OF CONSISTENCY

Ten players have made 100 or more consecutive league appearances for the Blades. In common with most clubs, goalkeepers prove to be the model of consistency in the form of Jack Smith, Ted Burgin and Alan Hodgkinson.

Jack Smith	206	1935–48 (includes war years without official games)
Alan Woodward	148	1967–72
Tony Currie	136	1968–72
Len Badger	126	1969–72
Jack Lievesley	125	1904–08
Derek Pace	119	1959–63
Brian Richardson	118	1960–64
Bob Cain	106	1894–98
Alan Hodgkinson	106	1965–68
Ted Burgin	102	1949–50

TIED IN KNOTS

As excuses go, Tony Currie's reason for failing to make the team after a goalscoring debut against Tottenham Hotspur was a good one. A week after netting with a header in late February 1968 he was getting married and his nuptials had been planned well in advance. Despite leaving the club in 1976 and trailing back to his native London for a spell, as well as Canada, he returned to Yorkshire during the 1980s and eventually took United's Football in the Community co-ordinator role. A post he has retained for over two decades.

THE COLOUR OF MONEY

Both Sheffield United's record fee paid and sum received stands at £4 million with Everton featuring in both deals. That sum was paid to the Merseysiders for James Beattie in August 2007. Exactly a calendar month earlier the same figure had been exchanged to obtain the services of centre-back Phil Jagielka. As part of that deal, the Blades were also given permission to talk over a move with Gary Naysmith whose eventual capture offset the deal.

The Blades have held the British transfer record only once when George Utley was recruited from Barnsley. The gargantuan sum of £2,000 had been exchanged and it almost doubled the club transfer record at the time. The subject – a replacement for Ernest Needham – came with the recommendation of Billy Gillespie who had come up against the one-time Sheffield Wednesday amateur plenty of times. Gillespie knew he was the player to have on board now the Blades' fortunes had dipped from the heady days of the late nineteenth and early twentieth centuries. An aggressive piece of transfer policy showed the board had no intention of letting things slip further and that if possible, the good times would return. A tough bargain struck by the clubs was followed by intensive negotiations with the player who received the offer of a longer term contract than was usual at the time – 5 years – and immediately gained the club captaincy.

Bolton Wanderers were offering fierce competition which ensured the sweeteners just kept coming. Also thrown in was the tenancy of a sports equipment shop which supplied the Blades and allowed extra money to come in. The deal took months to agree as a result. During this time the generosity increased and thrown in was the choice of a guaranteed £800 payment or a benefit comprising of the net receipts from a league game which Utley alone would select. Usually a testimonial was the best a player could hope to benefit from, though that would not happen unless many years of dedicated service had been put in. Utley opted for a share of the gate and selected a visit by Sunderland as the team who would provide it, allowing him to pocket £1,000. Though he earned his place in the first XI, a few quid was also earned by playing for the cricketing arm of Sheffield United. Utley's capture was a major factor in a reversal of fortune for United as a football team.

QUESTIONS IN THE HOUSE (OF COMMONS)

Alf Common was at one stage the Blades' record recruit costing £325 when snapped up from Sunderland in October 1901. The North-East outfit had been known as the 'team of all the talents' for much of the 1890s due to their quality in each position, and though Common couldn't help his team do better than runners-up spot in Division One, he was certainly a fine forward player. Earning an England cap plus a cup winners' medal after switching from inside forward to outside right for the replayed game at The Crystal Palace in 1902, proved he had plenty to offer United, but he grew restless and asked for a return to Roker Park. That was negotiated prior to the 1904/05 season commencing and marked the first £500-plus transfer in domestic football – the actual fee was £520 and included Blades keeper Albert Lewis who found himself sold on to Leicester Fosse within 9 months.

Common had already taken his leave by that point, departing to Middlesbrough for £1,000 in February 1905. That news was followed by a sharp intake of breath plus understandable mutterings from the Bramall Lane board seeing that they had allowed him a return after a series of attractive offers had been rejected. The player insisted business reasons lay behind his decision. United were unhappy at the situation but felt duty bound to honour the request. It was a bitter end to an otherwise glorious 3-year stay and something of a rebirth which allowed him to earn the type of reputation which justified a domestic transfer record. On a historical note, the deal that took Common from Sunderland to Middlesbrough led the Football Association to pass a rule limiting transfers between clubs to sums of no more than £350. Unworkable and largely ignored, it lasted just 3 months.

It took United another 5 years to shatter the £1,000 barrier themselves. Although this seems like chicken feed compared to current transfer records, when Commons exchanged hands at 4 figures it was termed as being 'flesh and blood for sale'. It even caused a stir in Parliament as one MP asked: 'Where will it all end?'

ON A COMMON THEME

Three years after the Alf Common affair, United found themselves effectively held ransom by another forward. Arthur Brown may not have enjoyed the same notoriety, but for a young man he had achieved an awful lot. He was a few weeks past his 17th birthday when awarded a debut and received an England cap the following year. Aged 18 years, 327 days he was the youngest player to be capped in that position. It was clear that this was a prodigious goalscoring talent who could achieve anything he wished in the game, especially at club level. He decided to reject any moves to stay at Bramall Lane in 1908 pleading for a return to his former club Gainsborough Trinity.

Claiming he wanted to devote more time to his family's business, he announced that if that particular move didn't transpire he would turn his back on the game. Once again the powers that be were unhappy at the situation but given the player's pledge to leave come what may, found their hands tied. Even a benefit which raised £232 failed to change his mind. The transfer back to Gainsborough never came off but he thought better of his threat when a move to Roker Park was organised just over a month later. Brown had only agreed to stay at the Lane if his contract became open to offers − £1,600 was at least some recompense to the club. His first game after joining Sunderland was against United at Bramall Lane and as most of his former admirers dreaded, he won the game scoring the only goal from the penalty spot. The following season he notched a hat-trick at the same venue. Fortunately United fans were spared any pain as it came in a FA Cup second round replay win over Brighton & Hove Albion.

FREE AND EASY MONEY

Every so often a player will be brought through the ranks or even picked up for a song after failing to turn heads elsewhere, then sold on for a huge profit. Marcus Bent is perhaps the best example. Recruited after his release by Port Vale, the striker who had failed to pull up too many trees at Vale Park or Crystal Palace suddenly hit a rich vein of form. A goal virtually every other game attracted the interest of Blackburn Rovers who had been embarrassingly relegated just 4 seasons after being crowned English champions. They had spent big to land that prize and were happy to do so again just to regain top-flight status. £2.1 million ended his 13-month stay at Bramall Lane. Fees totalling just over £10 million have so far been shelled out for the Londoner who was closing in on 500 career games when the 2009/10 campaign closed.

Others signed on free transfers who have gone on to fetch considerable sums when other teams have bid for their services include Georges Donis who joined from AEK Athens in March 1999. However, he was sold for £1 million to Huddersfield Town just under 3 months and 6 full appearances later. Dean Saunders was another player picked up for no fee which meant his £500,000 transfer to Benfica in December 1997 was all profit.

At the other end of the scale Adeola Akinbiyi has exchanged hands for £15.25 million and was United's one-time record purchase at £1.75 million when bought from Burnley in January 2006. Neil Warnock had bided his time, pursuing the player over the course of 18 months. Less than a year on, a £1 million loss was made when he went back to Turf Moor, just 4 goals, lengthy weight-lifting sessions in the gym and a training ground bust-up with Claude Davis being the footnotes of his stay.

POUND FOR POUND, A DECENT PLAYER

The most celebrated player in Chinese football, Hao Haidong, was signed from Dalian Shide for a mere pound early in 2005. There was an ulterior motive to the transfer. After an early foray into the Far East – prior to a formal expansion by the purchase of a club – there was a desire to get the 34-year-old in a coaching position. The press and player were told a place in the team was a real possibility before the forward dubbed the 'Chinese Alan Shearer' would return home to take part in the club's academy set-up in China. Injury put paid to his hopes of tasting English football before he joined the relatively newly acquired Chengdu Blades. It was the lowest transfer fee ever negotiated in world football until the record was broken when Chelsea gave PSV Eindhoven €1 in a specially constructed buy-out clause which allowed the Brazilian Alex to play in a good European league before his work permit could be sorted out. Taking into account the Euro exchange rate against sterling, the world's richest club at the time paid roughly 67p.

BY INVITATION ONLY

The Watney Mann Invitational Cup was a designed-for-television pre-season tournament organised between the sides that had scored the most goals in all four English Divisions. This was on the proviso that they had neither been promoted or had qualified for Europe. It ran over 4 years from 1970 and was sponsored by London-based brewers Watney Mann. United's 73 strikes over the 1970/71 season was more than any other Second Division team could muster and qualified them for a place in the 8-team event. A semi-final berth was achieved after a 6–0 win over Aldershot Town but a 1–0 defeat to Derby County in the last 4 ended the Blades' interest. A tally of 61 when the 1971/72 term concluded saw the Blades gain admission to the third tournament. Resounding wins over Notts County and Peterborough United earned them a place in the final. However, hosts Bristol Rovers won on penalties after a tense goalless draw.

BIRMINGHAM SILVER

Though the Birmingham Senior Cup is a competition for Midlands sides, United got a shot at the trophy and made the final in 1896 after beating Wolves, Walsall and Derby County. However, a powerhouse Aston Villa side ensured the cup would remain in the city which bore its name. The Blades were not invited to participate in subsequent seasons.

BLADES FLYING HIGH

The BOAC Cup was a one-off tournament in which United acquitted themselves. Somewhat unusually, all the matches were played against Blackpool in New Zealand at the close of the 1964/65 campaign. BOAC – the British Overseas Airways Corporation – was a state airline carrying out long-haul flights from the UK and the trophy was something of a publicity drive. The Seasiders took on United over 11 games with the winners being the team who recorded the most victories. United won 6 and consequently the trophy, plus a cheque for £1,000.

UPS ...

United are 1 of just 8 clubs to achieve a promotion in their first year of league football. Finishing second in Division Two led to a test match with Accrington who had ended next to bottom of the top flight at Nottingham. Jack Drummond grabbed the only goal of the game after surging down the left and beating 2 players before hitting an unstoppable shot. The Blades have also yo-yoed between divisions for much of the postwar years: 7 promotions and relegations were made between the highest 2 divisions between 1949 and 1976. A further half-dozen ups and downs occurred in the decade separating the end of the 1970s and 1980s. That included a dive down to the third tier.

Of the postwar promotions, the one earned at the end of the 1970/71 season was one of the most breathtaking any club could hope to manage. United went into the last dozen games in a promising if unlikely place to contest the 2 places on offer. Cardiff City, Carlisle United and Hull City all looked better-placed to follow champions-elect Leicester into the top flight but a run of

6 wins and 5 draws saw the Blades finish on 56 points, 3 ahead of third-place Cardiff.

United have managed to get themselves involved in 3 play-off tournaments. A first came in 1987/88 when the Blades finished 21st in Division Two. They were relegated to Division Three by virtue of a 2–1 aggregate defeat to Bristol City. By the time United next worked themselves into the competition, they were used to decide promotion issues only. Finishing fifth in the new First Division set-up, there was a semi-final with Ipswich Town at the close of the 1996/97 season. The aggregate scores were level at 3–3 after 2 games, but as the leg at Portman Road finished 2-apiece, the Blades went through on away goals. In the Wembley final Crystal Palace triumphed 1–0 and gained promotion to the Premiership. To compound United's misery, the winning goal came in the last minute. Twelve months later United were back in the picture despite finishing one place lower than they had a year earlier. Peter Reid's highly fancied Sunderland proved too tough, just: the aggregate score was 3–2.

Including this unique style United have gained promotion 9 times, the tightest of which was achieved by virtue of goals scored after the 1983/84 campaign when Hull City, level on points and goal difference, were edged out by the extra 15 goals United had scored.

... AND DOWNS

United's demotion on the final day of the season in 1994 was particularly galling given that Everton came back from 2 goals down to beat Wimbledon, and that the Blades' 3–3 draw at Stamford Bridge proved insufficient because of that result. Chelsea levelled with not just the last kick of that game but the last ball to be kicked in anger that season. Even with Everton winning, had that late goal not been conceded, Ipswich Town would have taken the fall. United have been relegated 10 times. The first came in 1934 after the Blades had spent 38 consecutive years among the élite. A fight against the drop had been ongoing for most of the season and was finally confirmed by a defeat at Elland Road in April. The worst run of demotions came from the years 1976 to 1981 as the Blades slid from the First to the Fourth Division. The game which consigned United to that stint in the Football League's basement was played on 2 May 1981. United were taking on the only other team that could have gone down in their place – Walsall. The match was played at break-neck speed, full of tough challenges and commitment. Don Givens would have averted the indignity had he converted a penalty with 2 minutes remaining. He missed and Walsall won 1–0 having scored from the spot 3 minutes earlier. A draw ensured Walsall finished a single place and a tantalising 1 point above the Blades. Then boss Martin Peters later revealed that Givens was not the club's nominated penalty taker but volunteered when the colleague given that duty declined due to the tension. Another interesting feature of the game was that the Blades went down with a positive goal difference, albeit +2, becoming only the second team in league history to achieve that dubious feat.

Essentially a penalty also saw the Blades relegated from the Premier League in May 2007. The season's final game at Wigan Athletic would decide which team went down. The odds were slightly stacked in United's favour. Anything but a defeat would see them through and send the Latics down. All seemed to be going well. The first half was winding to an end when a spot-kick was awarded for a Phil Jagielka handball. Substitute David Unsworth, who had joined the Lancashire side on a free transfer from Bramall Lane only 4 months earlier, converted from the spot. Danny Webber and Keith Gillespie both hit the woodwork during the second period. Even being a man up for the last 16 minutes failed to produce an equaliser. The Blades went down courtesy of having a goal difference one worse than their hosts.

TEVEZGATE

When the Blades were placed in the final Premiership relegation spot at the end of that 2006/07 season, there was a huge amount of controversy about the event. Though there were protests against clubs fielding weaker squads against other relegation candidates owing to other competitions being prioritised, West Ham United were saved by the exploits of Carlos Tevez. It had come to light that he and fellow Argentinian Javier Mascherano were owned by a third party rather than a club and no transfer fee had been paid to the previous teams the pair had served.

The situation was contrary to promises made by the Hammers. A record £5.5 million fine was handed out but the Blades, who failed to save themselves by avoiding defeat at Wigan on the last day, wanted a points deduction and were especially irate that Tevez had scored the goal which had saved West Ham. Attempts at legal and sporting redress failed, so moves were made towards financial recompense for the loss of a lucrative Premiership place. United were said to want anything up to £60 million and after almost 2 years of fighting were offered and accepted an out-of-court settlement totalling £20 million split into equal repayments over 5 seasons from the 2009/10 campaign.

WARNOCK'S PLAY-OFF TROUBLE

Although one of the most successful managers in play-off history, achieving 4 promotions via that route with Notts County, Huddersfield Town and Plymouth Argyle – and doing so in just 7 seasons – Neil Warnock failed to bring Sheffield United through the process twice. Under his charge the Blades were beaten in 2 finals on each occasion they were guided through, and they even failed to score. The 2002/03 season ended with a 3–0 defeat by Wolverhampton Wanderers in the final and marked the first time Warnock had been unsuccessful in the process. There was a direct promotion to the Premier League as Championship runners-up to Reading.

AN AWAY DAY EVERY WEEK

The Blades beat Wednesday to promotion by a single point at the close of the 1938/39 season, but as the campaign edged towards its conclusion, poor home form appeared likely to end hopes of rejoining the First Division. Boss Ted Davison decided he would mimick the usual conditions and preparations for away trips over the last 3 games at Bramall Lane. Consequently the players travelled out from Sheffield to Derbyshire by coach where they had a pre-match meal then returned; 2 wins and a draw were earned.

YOU WIN SOME, YOU LOSE MANY MORE

The Blades share a record for registering the fewest wins over the course of a campaign yet, in the era of two divisions or more, still survive relegation. The 1920/21 season saw United taste victory on just 6 occasions over the course of a 42-game campaign. That season two teams were relegated – Derby County and Bradford Park Avenue. The latter won 2 games more than the Blades but were half a dozen points worse off. Crystal Palace and Southampton also share the distinction.

THE HOTTEST OF HOTSEATS

Sheffield United have employed more managers than any other Football League club since 1945 when caretakers and other interim appointments are taken into account. Gary Speed's succession to Kevin Blackwell in August 2010 makes the former Welsh international United's 25th post-war boss.

PLAYING AGAINST THE ODDS

Republic of Ireland international David Kelly spent just 1 season at Bramall Lane and though far from the success he had been at other clubs, it is worth remembering that he had a career spanning somewhere in the region of 700 games. That's something which may have seemed unlikely when as a youngster he suffered from Perthes syndrome – a bone condition which kept his left leg 4 inches shorter than the right. It meant he walked with crutches for much of his childhood.

TIES TO ANOTHER COUNTRY

Former Blades midfielder Li Tie is one of China's most capped players though he played just 1 League Cup tie for Sheffield

United before he was transferred to sister club Chengdu Blades. Bryan Robson's decision to allow him the freedom to leave was reversed half a year before that move, but the 2001 Chinese Player of the Year failed to plot a way back to the first team when given that stay of execution. In 1993 along with other members of the Jianlibao youth team he was sent to Brazil for a 5-year training programme. The orders were from the Chinese government who hoped to build a formidable side for the turn of the next century and decided South America was the place to immerse their teenage prospects in the game. There they would be under the tutelage of Zhu Guanghu, who went on to coach the national side. Though the experiment may not have reaped the full desired outcome, it was deemed enough of a triumph to see other versions of the plan launched.

ANGLO-ITALIAN RELATIONS

Though they were League Cup winners, Third Division Swindon Town were not allowed to play in the Fairs Cup. As a consequence the Anglo–Italian Cup was born. It rewarded Swindon for their victory but also gave lower division sides a chance to earn a little extra finance by playing continental opposition. Within a few years of its inception, crowd violence forced the tournament to be scrapped only to be resurrected during the 1992/93 season. Top flight status exempted United until 1994 when they took on Serie B counterparts Udinese, Piacenza, Ancona and Cesena. A win, 2 draws and a defeat saw the Blades bow out at the group stage. That pretty much summed up the club's attitude to the competition which was scrapped once more a season later after complaints about fixture congestion and clubs being unable to agree dates.

BRIEF CAREERS

Lilleshall graduate John Ebbrell served Everton for just over a decade, though was primarily a bit-part player at Goodison, failing to live up to the potential shown during his early career. However, around the early 1990s he became an important part of the Merseysiders' midfield and a well-regarded character among the fans. His transfer to Bramall Lane for £1 million in February 1997 marked a new start for a player who, then 27, should still have had many good years ahead of him. Having said that, his United career lasted just 45 minutes. In a 2–0 home win over Reading he was replaced at half-time by a former Everton team-mate, Don Hutchison. He was never to play again courtesy of an ankle injury and just before a 2-year deal expired, he announced his retirement.

IN A DIFFERENT LEAGUE

Although fully fledged members of Division One, United were also members of the United Counties League for the 1893/94 and 1894/95 seasons. Essentially it was a subsidiary competition which other clubs such as Sheffield Wednesday, Derby County, Nottingham Forest and Notts County also participated in alongside their Football League membership. United finished 4th in their first season, but the whole exercise was seen as nothing more than an unnecessary diversion and subsequently scrapped.

A STAR IN EACH DIVISION

Cultured forward Keith Edwards is one of the few players to have turned out for United in all four English pre-Premier League divisions and perhaps the most noted to do so. He had a great goalscoring record in each flight and averaged more than a goal every 2 games. His 36 goals during the 1981/82 Fourth Division campaign makes him the only United player to have not only have topped the divisional scoring charts, but to be the Football League's top scorer as well.

An ability to lose the markers sent out to keep him quiet made Edwards a tricky man to control. Able to finish off a move in style, the man who had 2 stints at Bramall Lane was without doubt one of the most skilful players to have turned out for the club in modern times.

SUNDAY TRADING

Restrictions on the use of power and the three-day week introduced during 1974 led the football authorities to introduce Sunday kick-offs. These limited the effects the power workers' actions had on the smooth running of the fixture lists. United managed to avoid falling foul of these rules during the period of emergency measures. TV requirements were the major factor in the Blades playing a league game on a Sunday for the first time. A Division Three clash with Bradford City was broadcast in the Yorkshire region on 8 May 1983. The Bantams were hosts and won 2–0.

LIGHTS, CAMERA
AND PLENTY OF ACTION

The first FA Cup final to be filmed in 1901 also featured the Blades. Tottenham Hotspur were the opposition on the day. In March 1954 United were involved in the first ever floodlit game to be broadcast on live television when the second half of a friendly game at Millwall was beamed into living rooms. There is a rival claim to that distinction, though: Tottenham hosted a match with Racing Club de Paris 6 months earlier, though the exact status of the broadcast is clouded. Certainly a continental audience got their chance to witness United play when a fixture with Auxerre was broadcast live on French TV in January 1991. The Blades lost 2–1.

The Blades were chosen to be the subject of a fly on the wall BBC documentary entitled *United,* which followed the club's progress throughout the 1989/90 season. Fortunately there was a happy ending to the show as the club were promoted as Second Division runners–up.

BACK TO SQUARE ONE

United were involved in the first game ever to be broadcast live from a football ground. BBC Radio covered the match at Arsenal's Highbury ground on 22 January 1927. The Division One match finished 1–1 and was hailed as ground-breaking. The *Radio Times* carried a map of the pitch broken into eight squares, each numbered to allow the listener to know where the play was at any time. When the ball reached the rear quadrant to the right of the grid, and often where a goal-kick was being taken or when a keeper received a backpass, the commentator stated the teams were back to square one – giving rise to the phrase which is now in common parlance. The goals came from squares seven and eight, United's Billy Gillespie netting from the higher number.

STUFFING IN THE FIXTURES

For many years professional footballers were forced to forego their tinsel and turkey in order to play games on Christmas Day. United's last festive fixture took place in 1958 against Grimsby Town and ended in a 2–1 victory for the Blades. Bramall Lane hosted its last Christmas game in 1956 when Lincoln City were the visitors. United also took the spoils on this occasion courtesy of a 2–0 win.

POINTING AWAY FROM BRAMALL LANE

Up to the close of the 2009/10 season United had played 2,200 league games on their travels, winning 578 and drawing 435. 1,087 have ended in defeat with 2,658 goals scored and 3,930 conceded. This record would amass 1,879 points if aggregates were carried over 105 seasons of football.

OUTSIDE FOOTBALL

Away from the sporting world, Bramall Lane has also hosted an event staged by Evangelist Billy Graham in 1985 and a Bruce Springsteen concert in 1988.

FANCY A DOUBLE?

The most doubles (wins in both home and away matches) ever achieved by a Blades side over the course of a season is 9 during the 1960/61 term.

SCORING FOR BOTH SIDES

Players managing to score for both sides in the same game are rare. It has happened just once in Sheffield United's history when Colin Franks, who scored 5 in the same game for Watford reserves, netted an own goal for Blackburn Rovers in a Second Division encounter on 25 September 1976.

TRAGEDY AT THE LANE

Fatalities during football games are thankfully seldom, though Frank Levick possibly died as a result of an incident against Newcastle United on New Year's Day 1908.

He broke his collar bone and while recovering developed pneumonia a month later. Other reports, all wrong, suggest in attempting to block an effort on goal he felt the full force of a shot so fierce that it forced his testicles up and, when they lodged in his abdomen, internal bleeding within the bowel caused cardiac arrest.

Sam Wynne, a recent signing for Bury at a club record fee of £2,500 died at Bramall Lane. Just 5 months into his Gigg Lane career on 30 April 1927, he collapsed while preparing to take a free-kick and was taken to the dressing room but sadly died of pneumonia not long after. The game was rightly abandoned with proceeds from the rescheduled fixture donated to the bereaved family – £680 was raised by the 15,000 present.

Though a short-lived career by definition, the physical nature of professional football means it can be shortened even further. Joe Lievesley essentially saw his career and life ended by injury. During a match he broke his collar bone and was stretchered off. After release from hospital he rested at home but a month later his injury got the better of him: it had caused complications from which he eventually died. Keeper, Ernest Blackwell, was forced to hang up his gloves before his time in September 1924 after being advised to retire on medical advice. He went into preaching full-time after this, having mixed his ecumenical duties with his football for many years.

A keeper who could have achieved so much more but for serious illness ending his career was Mel Rees, who came into the United side towards the close of the 1991/92 season. United had been without a regular number one for most of the season, with Tracey, Kite, Hartfield and Wainwright all trying out the gloves before the Welshman was given a chance. It proved nothing less than a baptism of fire away to Liverpool. Despite the Reds boasting the league's costliest forward line, Mel was in sterling form helping United achieve a deserved 2–0 win. During the remaining 7 games played he kept another 3 clean sheets in a run of 5 wins and 2 draws. The only game lost was the 3–2 defeat by Leeds United which ensured the championship went to Elland Road. The late surge in results pushed the Blades into the top half of the table, but that Leeds match proved to be Rees' final game. Not too long afterwards he was diagnosed with bowel cancer. He died in 1993 at the age of 26, just months after walking out at Wembley and saluting the fans before the all-Sheffield cup semi-final. Each summer the Mel Rees Tournament is contested at the Sheffield United academy to raise money for St Luke's Hospice.

PUTTING THEIR SHIRTS
ON THE BLADES

The advent of shirt sponsorship during the late 1970s opened up a new opportunity for the club to earn extra revenue. Although there have been no headline-grabbing multi-million pound deals struck, it has at least given businesses the chance to put their shirts on United's backs. Cantor's were the first to do so in 1979. A 2-year deal came to an end allowing Bentleys to take over until they were replaced. Both the latter sponsors chose to run their logos vertically. After 12 months they were replaced by Simonds, a local Renault dealership, from which time sponsors' names have moved to their more usual position across the players' jerseys.

Laver held by far the longest sponsorship, lasting for just under a decade from the beginning of the 1985/86 campaign to the end of the 1994/95 season. Local brewers Wards took over and sponsored the club until the 1998/99 campaign concluded, from which time United wore their own nickname across the team's shirts. The Midas Interactive Entertainment Group agreed a deal in time for the beginning of the 2000/01 season, while Desun, HFS Loans and Capital One had taken sponsorship for a couple of seasons at a time. Visit Malta, essentially a message from the Maltese Tourist Board, have followed and also lend their name to the part of Bramall Lane formerly known as the John Street Stand.

The Football League's decision to permit secondary sponsors across the back of shirts have allowed Valad and Capita to get their names mentioned.

There was a change for one game only during the 2009/10 season as the Blades and Owls, when meeting in the 125th Steel City derby, shared a sponsor. Malta's Tourism Authority agreed to replace their logo with that of the Sheffield Children's Hospital. Sheffield Wednesday had donated its shirt sponsorship to the hospital for 2 seasons in order to promote its vital work. The signed one-off shirts the Blades players wore were sold at auction on the internet raising £4,200 for the cause.

YOU SCRATCH OUR BACK …

In a drive to boost attendances early in their existence, the Blades allowed 3 local theatres to advertise performances they were staging. People walked around the pitch with sandwich boards and in return, mention would be made in the theatre programmes or via bioscope cinema projections of forthcoming United games. The *Sheffield Telegraph* accepted half-rates for promotional adverts, which in turn gave them the right to display bill posters of their editions around Bramall Lane. During the 1933/34 season 50 display notices were placed at local railway stations.

ENGLISHMEN BROUGHT FROM FOREIGN FIELDS

To date Trevor Ross is 1 of just 2 English-born players United have bought from a foreign club. Ross came from AEK Athens while Peter Ander was signed and then sold back to Tampa Bay Rowdies. Scotsman Jimmy Johnstone was signed from San José Earthquakes.

KABBA'S UNIQUE HAT-TRICK

Steve Kabba earned a rare distinction during the 2002/03 season, scoring for Sheffield United, Crystal Palace and Grimsby Town during the same season. He began the campaign at Selhurst Park, though was loaned out to Grimsby before a month was out, remaining until early November. After another outing for Palace he came to Bramall Lane in a £250,000 deal. He scored on debut in a 5–0 win at Bradford City. One of his early games for Grimsby was an impressive display against United. The Blundell Park club wanted to make the temporary deal they had permanent, but simply couldn't compete with the Blades' spending power. The local paper ran a campaign aimed at trying to persuade him to remain. Pull-outs were printed with 'Stay Steve', and supporters asked to hold them up prior to the game. That goodwill ran out when he scored in a 4–1 win at Blundell Park and celebrated in front of those same fans.

A sole strike for the London outfit and 6 goals with Grimsby added to a very creditable 11 from 32 games after his switch to South Yorkshire. A couple of cup semi-finals and a play-off final ended a very good season. Fitness problems and the difficulty of getting back meant loans became a feature of Kabba's remaining career. He joined Watford during January 2007 in a deal worth double his original cost and brought about slight controversy by being forced to sit out an important Premier League clash between the two. A clause in the deal made him ineligible to turn out for the Hornets as both sides battled relegation. It was against the competition rules – but no action was taken before or after the game which Sheffield United won 1–0. Both sides finished in the bottom 3. As FIFA regulations now forbid any player turning out for more than 2 teams in the same season, Kabba's goalscoring feat is one that cannot be equalled.

OLDEST ...

In first-class league and cup games the oldest players to turn out for United are:

Jimmy Hagan at 39 years and 236 days when he played his last game against former club Derby County on 14 September 1957.

Jack Pickering and Jack Smith trail in at 39 years and 14 days, then 39 years and 9 days respectively.

Just 2 players have made a first-team appearance for the Blades over the age of 40. They are Albert Sturgess and Billy Gillespie just before they left the club.

Reg Wright became the oldest United debutante when he took to the field against Doncaster Rovers on 28 September 1940, not long past his 39th birthday. The game was of course during the war, marking his first and only appearance for the club as he was actually a member of the coaching staff.

The oldest Football League debutante was former Wednesday player Joe Cockroft who sampled his first game for the Blades at the age of 37 years and 5 months on 6 November 1948 against Preston North End. Remarkably, despite his years at Hillsborough it was the first game Cockroft played in the top flight.

... AND YOUNGEST

Sheffield United's youngest ever starter participated in wartime football. Schoolboy international Dennis Thompson was just 16 years and 103 days old when given a chance to wear the red and white stripes. A promising, locally-produced forward, he was the club's joint top scorer when the 1947/48 campaign ended (with 11 strikes), but grabbed just 9 more league goals before joining Southend United in 1951. Afterwards he drifted into non-league football.

The youngest ever participant in a first-team game is Trenton Wiggan who came on as a substitute in a League Cup game with Doncaster Rovers not long before his 17th birthday. The youngest player ever to have started a league or cup game for the club was Stephen Hawes who made his debut at the tender age of 17 years and 47 days. Remarkably, including Hawes there are a cluster of 4 junior players whose ages when they made their league bows were within 22 days of that record. They are Julian Broddle at 17 years and 62 days, Gary Hamson at 17 years and 67 days and Tony Wagstaff who was 17 years and 69 days. Only the latter names went on to enjoy lengthy periods with the Blades.

FRIEND OR FOE?

Heeley Stokes was the first player to put through his own net against United, in the second qualifying round of the 1889/90 FA Cup. His goal helped set up a 2–0 win and put the Blades through for a tie in the next round. The first in the Football League came in a Division One game against Newton Heath, now more commonly known as Manchester United, on 25 November 1893. Goalkeeper Joseph Fall scored the own goal in a 3–1 win.

LONG AND DISTINGUISHED SERVICE

Jack Pickering spent 23 seasons with United, making him the longest-serving player in the club's history. Though even his contribution is dwarfed when compared to George Waller who spent 39 seasons at Bramall Lane – serving first as a player and then on the coaching staff. Cec Coldwell followed a similar career path and during his 32 years with the Blades was made acting manager twice. Initially it was for 9 days in 1975 between Ken Furphy and Jimmy Sirrell's stints. Then he managed the team over the best part of 4 months after Sirrell departed and prior to Harry Haslam taking command. Though Billy McEwan was officially appointed manager on 27 March 1986, Coldwell assisted and worked closely with him until the season closed.

WHEN DAVID SLAYED GOLIATH

In the FA Cup, United hold a fairly decent record against non-league opponents with most of the defeats to teams outside the Football League structure coming during the early part of the twentieth century when the standard of non-league football was every bit as good as that within the professional realm. Those non-league teams to have beaten the Blades are: Port Vale who were first round winners in 1897/98; Tottenham Hotspur who became the only non-Football League side to win the FA Cup courtesy of beating Sheffield United in 1901; Swindon Town, a real force in the Southern League who overcame the Blades during the 1907/08 season; and Darlington who, a decade before their entry into the league, emphasised their credentials with a 1–0 win at the opening stage in the 1910/11 competition. The only non-league outfit to beat United in recent times are Altrincham. The

Cheshire-based part-timers were on the edge of claiming a spot in the Football League when they disposed of the Blades in the 1981/82 competition after a replay. In truth there was very little difference between the teams in terms of league placings at that point, around 30, with United in the Fourth Division and aiming for promotion above all other prizes.

BANKING ON BARCLAY

An attack-minded midfielder, Bobby Barclay bagged 77 goals from the 264 games he played for United over 6 years. That number could have been swelled had he not been so unselfish when presented with a chance. If Barclay thought a colleague was better placed to find the net, he would usually attempt to get the ball to them. He had cost £3,500 from Derby County and linked up well with the 2 forwards who had led the line so well for United – Jimmy Dunne and Jock Dodds. Both already-prolific marksmen found their goals to games ratio soar after the introduction of Barclay to the side. Top-half finishes over his first 2 seasons could have been improved had United not been so prone to conceding goals, but at the close of the 1933/34 term those frailties at the back saw United finish bottom of the First Division.

JOCK'S AWAY

Allowing Jock Dodds to join Blackpool just months prior to the 1938/39 season being completed may have seemed an odd decision. Especially as the forward, who averaged a goal in just under every two games, had netted his 100th league strike for the promotion-chasing Blades just months earlier and would have been a useful spearhead in the top flight. However, the Scot had sought a move to Lancashire for family reasons which a grateful United board were happy to comply with. No doubt £10,000 – the second-highest transfer fee ever paid by an English club – proved useful in their decision making process, too. Dodds had cost nothing when picked up from Huddersfield Town 4 years earlier. It was money well spent for the Seasiders who saw the investment come up trumps with 10 goals. All were vital strikes which helped them escape relegation from Division One.

OFFSIDE RULE BENEFITS BLADES

In 1925 the FA changed the offside rule slightly meaning just 2 players had to stay goalside of an attacker taking the ball rather than 3. A consequence was to increase the number of goals scored, as offside traps had been far too rigid for strikers to break down and games could be ruined by defensive tactics, plus a large number of free-kicks. The Blades were top-scorers on the first day the new law was applied putting 11 past Cardiff City on 1 January 1926. The Welsh club were only able to muster a couple in reply. Across the leagues most teams were able to register bigger results. By way of illustration, 4,700 goals were scored over the previous campaign across 1,848 games. The number subsequently increased to 6,373.

DRAWING CONCLUSIONS

United's highest scoring draw is the 5–5 result with Leicester City at Filbert Street on 3 November 1951. The Blades led 4–3 at half time but were pegged back by the home team. Outside the league, sharing 8 goals with Liverpool in an FA Cup semi-final replay at Burnden Park marks the heaviest tied score. The Blades went through when the two sides reconvened, but had it not been for a Peter Boyle own goal and Jack Cox managing to pick up the pieces after Willie Foulke saved a penalty, another attempt would not have been needed. Liverpool twice held a lead but simply couldn't keep those advantages.

The most draws the Blades have ever amassed over a season is 18 from 42 games in the 1920/21 season with the fewest stalemates played out being 2 during the 1904/05 season. Just 34 games comprised a season back then. Over the more usual 42-game campaign, the lowest number of draws recorded is 5 (from the 1951/52 and 1969/70 campaigns).

SEQUENCES OF EVENTS

Eight straight league wins have been recorded 5 times and this sequence stands as a club record. First set in the late winter and spring of 1893, it was last equalled at the beginning of the 2005/06 promotion season. 22 games passed without a loss between September 1899 and mid-January 1900, though only 5 consecutive victories were registered in that period as the Blades remained unbeaten from the season's opening day until journeying to Bury. A 2–1 defeat rocked the then leaders, and another 3 defeats and 4 draws from the 11 games remaining allowed defending champions Aston Villa to nip in and retain their crown with a 2-point margin. It was a massive pick-up from the 16th place occupied a season earlier, but a huge disappointment given that their destiny was very much in the team's own hands.

A DISASTROUS
DEBUT

Goalkeeper Lee Baxter spent his career playing extensively in his native Sweden, only leaving for brief spells with Rangers and then a month with Sheffield United midway through the 2003/04 season. The son of Wolverhampton-born (but Scottish-raised) Stuart Baxter, he was drafted in due to an acute crisis between the posts.

Paddy Kenny was out with a long-term knee injury and Paul Gerrard returned to Everton after a 3-month loan expired, 23-year-old Kristian Rogers (who had appeared shaky in his League Cup debut at Queens Park Rangers just under two months earlier) was the sole but unpreferred option. In his only game, at Burnley, Lee Baxter fumbled a shot into his own goal after just 17 minutes then allowed a header which seemed to require only a routine save to squirm beneath him just past the half-hour mark. For these troubles he was substituted at half time and failed to appear in Neil Warnock's plans before heading back to Malmö.

The manager had been seeking to land Birmingham City's Ian Bennett and later confessed he knew little about his Scandinavian acquisition. Alan Fettis, who was also signed just before the game to provide back-up, came on. United had gained the lead before the second lapse but went on to lose 3–2, Robbie Blake grabbing a penalty on the stroke of half time. Baxter bore no responsibility for the foul and was helpless to avert the spot-kick. Bennett was loaned to the Blades during the next campaign as Paddy Kenny was again ruled out and joined on a permanent basis when United reached the Premier League in 2006.

FUELLING AMBITION

A competition sponsored by the American oil company Texaco pitted English, Irish and Scottish teams with no European commitments against each other over the course of a season. United chose not to enter over its first 2 years but did make an appearance during the 1972/73 campaign by which time Ireland's representatives had pulled out. Matches were contested over 2 legs and West Bromwich Albion were the Blades' first opponents. A 1–1 draw at Bramall Lane with Tony Currie grabbing the goal followed by 1–0 home win at The Hawthorns secured Albion's passage through to the next round. A season on, Dundee United were the first-round opposition. They too held the Blades to a home draw, this time 0–0, before winning the tie in their home leg. The score north of the border was 2–0.

Group stages were introduced for the start of the 1974/75 season which did at least allow United to face more than one side. However, their record was just as woeful as in previous terms. Despite recording a first win in the competition against Manchester City, that 4–2 home victory proved their last. Oldham Athletic hammered United 4–2 at Boundary Park and Blackpool edged the Blades out 2–1 at Bramall Lane. The sponsorship deal expired at the end of the season at which time the competition became known as the Anglo-Scottish Cup. United's record from that point remained far from impressive. The initial matches were played over mini-leagues during the pre-season, in order to act as useful friendlies. Only once did the Blades manage to extend their interest into the season proper and the knockout phase. That was in the 1979/80 competition.

ARE THE KIDS ALRIGHT?

United have a fairly average record in the premier knockout competition for junior players, the FA Youth Cup, with a semi-final berth in 1973 being their best achievement. United's youngsters were edged out 2–1. The best score ever recorded in the competition was the 16–0 demolition of Doncaster Rovers in October 1968.

THE HOUDINI CLUB

Calling United a Houdini club is perhaps a trite description of the Blades' miraculous escapes from the clutches of relegation during the early 1990s. Yet it is an apt one. The nickname was bestowed on Dave Bassett's team towards the end of the 1990/91 season when, after appearing certainties for the drop following a dismal start, United avoided what had been deemed a certain relegation with ease. Sixteen games (over a third of the season) had passed and United had just 5 points. They were the only club in all 4 divisions without a win to their name. The Blades, who had established a top-flight record for the most dismal start to a season, and one which still stands, remained bottom of the pile until after Christmas – many points adrift of safety. For his part Bassett dismissed the prophets of doom but it all seemed nothing more than just talk and fighting the good fight.

The signings of Vinnie Jones and Brian Marwood were seen as last-gasp attempts to dig the club out of a hole – or at least limit the depths they could plummet to. As Jones had spirited if rudimentary on-field leadership and Marwood an ability to create goals from the wings, the ploy had merit. Especially the latter considering the strengths of Brian Deane and Tony Agana in the area. Even so there seemed little chance of success. The ship started to turn round in the 17th league game when United recorded their first victory. It may have been a narrow 3–2 win over Nottingham Forest but it was 3 points and proved the start of the biggest comeback since Lazarus. Over the next 20 games United won 12 (including 7 in a row) and drew 3, earning 39 points out of 60. These feats lifted the club 5 places and a dozen points above the drop zone.

These events and similar miraculous escapes led Bassett to hold the club's Christmas party before the 1992/93 season kicked off as his team only seemed to perform after the festive season had closed. This type of man-management may well indicate the real reason why the Blades were able to survive as long as they did. When the inevitable did catch up with the club in 1994, it more or less spelled the end of an era. Despite their top-flight place looking in doubt most seasons, United showed great FA Cup form having reached the quarter-finals in 1990 and the semi-finals in 1993.

Just before Christmas 1995 Bassett resigned his post. United had finished eighth in Division One the previous term but rarely looked likely to gain promotion. A change of personnel in the boardroom as Mike McDonald took over as club chairman seemed to make up Bassett's mind for him.

ASSOCIATE MEMBERSHIP

The 1980s had seen English clubs turn away from the continental model of modest-sized leagues and one low-key cup competition. However, as teams in the bottom two divisions were keen to bump up the number of games played, there were moves to introduce a small-scale knockout cup for the lower ranks. Consequently, for the 1983/84 season the Associate Members'

Cup was born. United's only appearance in the trophy was under its original guise and in its initial season. Split into North and South sections consisting of 24 teams in each group, United made the semi-finals without straying too far from home. After beating Rotherham United, Bradford City and Scunthorpe United they were edged out by Hull City in the last four. It may seem impressive but, all in all, the competition was just a distraction. The club were happy to keep it at arm's length after gaining promotion from the Third Division – courtesy of goals scored after finishing level with Hull.

A MOUNTAIN OF A MAN

The Edwardian age was not the most politically correct era of history, so regular references to keeper William Foulke as 'Fatty' were perhaps viewed very differently to how they may be perceived now. The Shropshire-born stopper was, and remains, the heaviest player to ever to participate in professional football. Given the physical standards of the modern game he will undoubtedly remain so. With the Blades, Foulke won an English championship and 2 FA Cup winners' medals. He was always a big man, tipping the scales at 15 stones at the onset of his career but ballooned his way to the 22-stone mark by the time he hung up his gloves. Some speculation suggests he actually added a few more pounds and tipped the scales nearer 25 stones. While playing in a match between the Sheffield and Derbyshire leagues, he caused play to be held up by deciding to swing on a crossbar which promptly broke. When he tore a muscle making a save during another game and needed to be carried off, there were no stretchers big enough. For that event 6 men were called upon to discharge the awesome duty. Although a weighty man, his bulk was disguised by his height. He stood well over 6ft tall, wore size 12 boots and took a 24in collar on his shirts. His power was marvelled at by crowds and he was rumoured to kick and punch balls further than any other keeper. His fists often propelled the ball to the halfway line.

A programme note once stated: 'Foulke says he doesn't care how much they [forwards] charge him, so long as they don't charge him too much for his dinner.' Despite that happiness at being worked by those seeking to beat him, his short fuse was legendary. He also sought to devour a striker's all-important confidence with as much relish as he regarded meal times. Very few men would feel tempted to argue with him. When forwards did, they would normally come out second best. In October 1898 Liverpool's George Allan found this out the hard way when, after trying a shoulder barge, he found himself unceremoniously picked up and dunked head-first into the mud. United led 1–0 at the time. Andrew McCowie converted the resulting penalty and Allan had the last laugh by scoring the winner. This was by no means an isolated incident. On another occasion an opposing striker was grabbed by the waist and thrown into the net. He took to the stands one afternoon to remonstrate with Sheffield Wednesday fans who were cat-calling him. It is even said that he napped during some matches when left with very little to do. The incident with Liverpool may explain the animosity that seemed to be present between United keeper Billy Foulke and Rab Howell when United met Liverpool the following season. The fact that Howell was a former team-mate held no sway, nor did the occasion or the identity of those incurring his wrath.

The 1902 FA Cup final's first game finished 1–1 courtesy of an equaliser 2 minutes from time. Foulke raged at what he considered to be the highly debatable circumstances in which Harry Wood netted. Southampton's captain had been crouched tying up his bootlaces in an offside position but it was decided a touch on the shorts of a Sheffield defender played him onside. While enjoying his post-match bath, the keeper took it upon himself to protest with the officials. Stark naked he emerged from the dressing room forcing referee Tom Kirkham to seek refuge in a broom cupboard. Had it not been for a party of FA officials, those present suggest the doors would have been torn from their hinges. The stopper had a point and many years later Edgar Chadwick, who had sent the ball through for Wood, confessed there had been no touch on his pass. Tempers had soothed by the replay 7 days later, though the Burslem official was probably glad United emerged victorious.

Stories regarding this literally larger-than-life character are plentiful. At Bradford, a last posting and a final season, his red jersey clashed with that of Accrington Stanley. There wasn't an alternative choice large enough to encapsulate his bulk so a bed sheet was procured from a nearby residence. He was said to arrive for meals with team-mates early and prior to his colleagues turning up, enjoy food which had been laid out for the squad. During his time with Chelsea he saved 2 penalties in a game with Burton Albion, the taker suggesting he could do little more than direct the ball close to the stopper as: 'There was nowhere else to aim!'

After Foulke finished playing he was alleged to have earned money on Blackpool's seafront with a 'beat the keeper' attraction for those who felt confident enough to try their luck. Other unsubstantiated stories include one which says that it was on the Fylde Coast, while scratching a living on an extremely chilly day, that he is said to have died aged 42 after contracting pneumonia. Or possibly not. Other accounts suggest he was the landlord of a Sheffield pub and at another time ran a corner shop – presumably able to resist eating his stock. Whatever the truth, Foulke may have agreed with the newspaper editor played by Carleton Young in *The Man Who Shot Liberty Valance* who said: 'When the legend becomes fact, print the legend.'

BIRTH OF THE BALL BOY

Foulke's heft inadvertently gave rise to the creation of ball boy roles for youngsters during games. On leaving Bramall Lane he joined Chelsea for £50. To ensure he wasn't troubled by the task of retrieving shots and headers which evaded him, the Pensioners gave two youngsters the job of standing behind his goal in order to field stray efforts. Often the boys on duty would sprint to fetch the ball when it went out of play in other areas and this was copied by other clubs to ensure games were speeded up.

TINY MEN, GREAT KEEPERS

By contrast to Willie Foulke, United have fielded some of the smallest keepers to have stood between the posts. Foulke left very little of the goal for strikers to find either side of his bulk, but Alan Hodgkinson standing 5ft 9in and his immediate predecessor Ted Burgin (2 inches shorter), gave plenty of scope for the high ball. However, both were able to compensate more than adequately. Between them they occupied the goal line between 1949 and 1971, only allowing deputies a handful of opportunities in the eventuality of injuries, and made a combined total of 989 appearances.

WINNING ON POINTS

United's record tally over the course of a season under the 2 points
for a win system is 60 from the 1952/53 Division Two campaign.
When wins were rewarded by 3 points, United amassed 96 during
the 1981/82 season when the Fourth Division championship was
claimed.

QUICK-FIRE BLADES

The best example of heavy and rapid scoring by the team came
during the 6–2 win over Newcastle United on 1 January 1955.
United were 4–0 up after just 8 minutes and led 5–2 at half time.

NATURAL BALL-PLAYERS

There are a lucky few who can turn out at the highest levels in
more than one sport. United seem to have more than a fair share
of able cricketers. Prime among them must be Wally Hardinge,
who often acted as a talismanic inside-forward for the Blades and
played county cricket for Kent. He could be termed a mercurial
footballer as despite his immense talent he could as often be
shockingly awful or superb. A football international he was only
capped as an England cricketer after his soccer career ended and
he returned south. Willie Foulke appeared for Derbyshire in the
odd first-class game, taking 2 wickets for 15 runs in one match
and managing a half century. Ernest Needham was a more regular
feature for the same county as a decent left-handed batsmen,
moderate right-armed bowler and occasionally a wicket-keeper.
Jack Chisholm played a match for Middlesex against Oxford

University during his time at Brentford but otherwise enjoyed a career in the minor counties for 11 summers.

Ted Hemsley donned whites and scored such a tremendous amount of runs that he came close to gaining a Test cap. The left-back is 1 of only 2 men to play football and cricket at Bramall Lane. He occupied the home dressing room with the Blades and the away one as a right-handed batsman and occasional bowler with Worcestershire. Yorkshire County Cricket Club and Sheffield United have shared just one employee – Willie Wilkinson, a left-handed bat and infrequent orthodox finger spinner who turned out at the Lane almost as often for Yorkshire as he did for the Blades; 17 of his 127 first class games were at the venue.

COURTING SUCCESS

Though he only spent a little over a month on loan at Bramall Lane, Manchester-born but Sheffield-raised Michael Boulding should be added to any list of gifted sportsmen. He was a very talented tennis player as well as a footballer and opted for that sport in his teens after being scouted by a member of Stefan Edberg's coaching team. He played in many minor tournaments as well as competing for the boys' championship at Wimbledon plus qualifiers for Grand Slam tournaments. Though a contemporary of Tim Henman, he only managed to peak at 1,119 in the world rankings due to the limited number of matches played, though that did place him in Britain's top 20. Many would counter that is a limited achievement given the dearth of talent in the country during the late 1990s. His links with football had been maintained throughout this period with Hallam FC. Joining Mansfield Town as a professional saw him turn away from tennis and set his sights on a sport with very different references to nets and Wimbledon.

BOXING CLEVER

Graham Shaw, who ranks as one of the best players in United history and almost certainly the club's finest half-back, was an excellent junior cricketer who played for Yorkshire Colts. However, his future wasn't about a two-way sporting battle. There remained another option. He was a boxer and an English ABA junior champion.

TRADING THE PITCH FOR BLOWS

In contrast, Curtis Woodhouse went from the pitch to the boxing ring. The midfielder made over a century of appearances for Sheffield United and acquired 4 England Under-21 caps but left all that behind in 2006 to become a pugilist. The midfielder claimed to have 'fallen out of love with the game', but continued to turn out in the non-league arena and lower echelons of the Football League as well as plying his trade as a light welterweight. A winner in his first bout, the 'Driffield Destroyer' as he is known, most recently turned out for Sheffield FC. Woodhouse has fought at Bramall Lane twice and the Sheffield United academy on one occasion.

SUBBING MARKS

Andrew Scott has made the most substitute appearances in a United shirt. He made 39 league starts but was introduced as a replacement on 36 occasions. In all competitions the total of introductions during a game rises by 2 and his total appearances reach 49.

Officially substitutes were allowed to sit on the team bench from 21 August 1965. It took United 3 weeks to exploit the rule by introducing Tony Wagstaff for Alan Birchenall on 8 September 1965 during a Football League game at Fulham. Ken Mallender became the first replacement to score, on 25 April 1965. Arsenal were visitors to Bramall Lane that day and the goal was the last scored in a comprehensive 3–0 win. Only one substitute has managed to score a hat-trick after joining the fray. That was Keith Edwards in the second round second leg League Cup tie with Grimsby Town. From the 1986/87 season 2 substitutes were allowed to be named which eventually allowed Peter Duffield to become the first substitute to be substituted when he was replaced by Dane Whitehouse in a Third Division game with Fulham on 29 April 1989.

Steve Neville claimed the most notorious of records when he became the first number 12 to be sent off in a league match with Scunthorpe United.

Rules allowing the replacement of injured players or tactical changes during a game are a relatively modern innovations but technically Willie Mosforth was used in this way as far back as November 1899 when he covered for George Aizlewood who was late in arriving for the game against Bolton Wanderers. Mosforth played for no more than a couple of minutes but as the game was a friendly the switch could be made by the agreement of both captains.

KEEPING UP APPEARANCES

Carl Muggleton was the first substitute goalkeeper used, although not in exchange for a fellow custodian. He was actually introduced as an outfield replacement and played out the last few minutes of a league game with Reading in April 1996. As he was only on a month's loan cover from Leicester City, chances were limited and it proved to be his only game in a United shirt.

Charles Sutcliffe enjoyed a fairytale ending to his career when he joined the Blades in 1924. The club faced something of a goalkeeping crisis following the enforced retirement of Ernest Blackwood and Harold Gough's decisions to leave football. The 33-year-old Sutcliffe had been keeping goal for lowly Rotherham United in the Third Division and was viewed by many as nothing more than a regulation lower-league stopper. Yet just under 6 months later he was turning out in and playing a major part in United's fourth FA Cup triumph. With his brother John he holds the record for a longest period between 2 siblings appearing in an FA Cup final. Both kept goal, with John turning out for Bolton Wanderers – defeated by Notts County – in the 1894 final; 31 years on Charles was part of the Blades XI which beat Cardiff City in the 1925 final.

CAREER DEVELOPMENT PROGRAMME

Until 1897 the match day programme took the form of a simple card listing the expected line-up and a season's remaining fixtures. United player Billy Whitham topped up his soccer earnings by selling these and cricket scorecards during the summer months. After this date a programme similar to the modern-day edition – *The Blade* – was published. Initially consisting of 8 pages, it also detailed the day's teams and remaining fixtures as well as general items such as theatre reviews and adverts. Photographs were added just before the First World War. During the 1930s pagination increased to 20 pages. A full colour cover was introduced 5 years into the new decade.

Paper rationing during both world wars saw the programme reduce to a single folded piece of paper. It returned to the booklet style following the Allied victory, even if a little shorter in page numbers. The programme has kept pace with the rapidly increasing upturn in the club's affluence and the quality of technology available to publishers. This has seen it grow into a something resembling a mini-magazine over the intervening years with full colour introduced in the 1980s.

UNBEATABLE

United have failed to lose against Burton United, Darlington, Glossop North End, Halifax Town, Hartlepool United, Hereford United, Northampton Town, Northwich Victoria, Rochdale, Torquay United and York City. The fact that some of these teams have now lost their league status or gone out of existence of course means they will probably never beat the Blades. Only Cambridge United and Shrewsbury Town have never lost a league game to United. However, Cambridge were beaten in an Anglo-Scottish Cup encounter and Shrewsbury have been defeated in the League Cup.

Peterborough United would have been added to that list of winless sides but for a victory in March 2010 – Posh's first in 8 attempts. Their best result prior to that had been a League Cup draw during September 1984: at least the scores were tied after 90 minutes . . . the Blades gained a winner in extra-time.

TOUR OF DUTY

United's first tour in Europe was of Denmark shortly after the 1936 FA Cup final.

FAMILY AFFAIRS

Footballing skills often tend to run in families. Large dynasties of professionals can trace a lineage back over many generations. United are no different, boasting a number of siblings – many of whom have played in the same sides – plus sons following their fathers as Bramall Lane alumni. Peter and Tommy Boyle were among the first within that latter category. Peter signed for United in 1898 from Sunderland and was an Irish international for many years. Though his son couldn't emulate his father in terms of international caps, he did earn an FA Cup winners' medal with the Blades in the 1925 final. His father had lifted the trophy in his debut season.

Harry Johnson senior and junior equalled that feat in 1902 and 1925. The right-back became a member of the coaching staff upon hanging up his boots, from where he had the perfect position to see sons Harry and Tom proudly make their debuts. The younger Harry Johnson wrote many pages in the United history books by becoming the club's record scorer with a mark which remains unbeaten. Tom possibly found the shadow created by his father and brother hard to live in. Despite this he was a versatile player who switched from wing-half to the centre of defence, but ultimately failed to cement a position in the squad and saw little more than a couple of dozen games spread over 5 seasons but did play in a cup final – albeit to claim only a runners-up medal in 1936.

Ten other sets of brothers, mostly pairs, have turned out for Sheffield United at various grades, the most recent being Alan, Keith and Stephen Quinn, who have all been on the club's books, though only the latter two have played in the same side. Keith never managed a senior outing before leaving the Blades in 2009.

Most of the Sampy brothers signed during the 1920/21 season. Tommy was a busy right-sided midfield player who always contributed his all to the cause, but ultimately was left bitter by his treatment from the selectors. Prime among his grievances was exclusion from the 1925 FA Cup-winning side. Having played in both the quarter- and semi-final games he must have fancied his chances of making an appearance at Wembley. However, despite Tommy Boyle not being a regular feature in the side, he had given a good account of himself in each opportunity offered and was preferred on the day. Bill Sampy's career scaled few heights and throughout most of his 6 years at Bramall Lane he was nothing more than a fringe player. Arthur Sampy joined the club within a year of the 1925 cup win and lined up in close proximity to his sibling Bill at inside-right. Over 2 seasons, the pair found themselves in the same XI just under 40 times but were both told they should look for another club in 1928.

Barry and Tony Wagstaff were successful graduates of United's far-sighted youth policy instituted during the 1950s, but which really began to bear fruit the following decade.

Bernie Wilkinson never signed full professional terms as a footballer, preferring to retain his job in the poultry trade as well as play. He always shunned attempts to lure him, even though he could probably have staked a claim to a regular spot in the line-up. Despite that reticence to commit himself full-time, he succeeded Ernest Needham to the captaincy where he continued to inspire all those around him and was awarded international caps. The defender was actually a very gifted cricketer to boot and turned down many invitations made by United's co-residents at Bramall Lane, Yorkshire County Cricket Club. His brother Willie did take up similar offers as well as a contract with the Blades but lacked the full extent of his sibling's ability as a footballer. He made a limited number of appearances at inside-forward and also turned out for United's cricket club, with whom he scored a number of runs owing to his hard hitting of the ball. Bernard gave up skippering the side in 1912 and was released to join Rotherham Town. After retiring he remained a resident of Sheffield until his death in May 1949. David and A. Mercer, Andy and Rob Scott, Brian and Paul Smith, Tommy and Jamie Hoyland, Colin and Lee Morris make up the rest of the compliment of brothers to have joined United.

Arthur Brown became a Blade in May 1902 after a whirlwind start to his career. After just 3 games with Gainsborough he had scored 2 goals. That was enough to persuade the Bramall Lane board to take their chance on the country's hottest youngster. His pace and shooting ability were among his main attributes but in conjunction with his skill on the ball and eye for an opening, it made him a truly great player. Exactly a century of goals came from his 178 Football League outings and his magnificent scoring ratio of roughly a goal every other game was maintained in the cup where he scored 4 from 9 games. His brother Fred played for United initially as a guest during the First World War, subsequently signing full-time after the hostilities ceased.

Former Manchester United player Lou Macari took a place on the coaching staff when invited to join the club by Steve Bruce. Lou's son Paul spent a few years on United's books but made very little impact and was released in April 2000. Outside first-class league and cup games, Steve Ludlam saw his son Ryan turn out in some friendly fixtures, as did Ken Furphy who gave his son Keith a run out while manager.

HARRY'S INAUSPICIOUS START

Dave Bassett joined the Blades midway through the 1987/88 campaign. Try as he might, 'Harry' as he was known throughout the game, couldn't lift Watford away from the First Division's relegation zone – an area they had occupied since the early weeks of the campaign – and was sacked. United occupied a position somewhere close to mid-table a rung below. Just a matter of days after he left Vicarage Road, Bassett's chance came at Bramall Lane due to Billy McEwan's resignation. The smart money would have been on his old and new sides meeting in Division Two a season later but Bassett didn't prove a such steady hand at the tiller. A dip in results from January onwards saw the Blades plummet to the third tier after defeat to Bristol City in the new-fangled relegation play-offs. However, though he became one of very few managers to lead 2 different clubs to relegation in the same season, he guided the Blades to successive promotions and a place in the top flight during his 393-game stint as manager.

NO SHAVING UNTIL WEMBLEY

United have fielded a number of hirsute players over the years. Tony Currie possessed prodigious sideburns and Trevor Hockey had a fine beard – not to mention that Beatles haircut. But only Alan Cork has grown the full set of whiskers to directly aid the cause rather than as a fashion statement. Or at least that's how the striker saw it during the 1992/93 FA Cup run. After Burnley were beaten in a third round replay he refused to take a razor in hand until the road to Wembley was blocked. Cork played beneath the twin towers but only as a semi-finalist. It was of course Sheffield

Wednesday who won the last-four tussle and went on to play Arsenal. Almost 4 months of growth was whipped off soon after.

HOME SWEET HOME

The club's record for successive home wins is 11 in all matches during the 1890/91 season. Up to the close of the 2009/10 campaign United had played 2,200 league games at Bramall Lane winning a highly impressive 1,177 of them. 555 ended in draws with 468 in defeat. 4,109 goals were scored in the process with 2,433 conceded. Carried through to percentages, that winning ratio represents a 53.5 per cent success rate.

FIELD DRESSING – BLADES IN THE FA CUP

United have won the FA Cup 4 times with their first victory in 1899 achieved by an excellent team display which saw off a very competent Derby County. The Rams held a 1–0 half-time lead and Harry Thickett took part in the showpiece, wearing an estimated 50-yards of bandages plus stiffened canvas to protect broken ribs and ruptured muscles in his side. He was rumoured also to have taken a few tots of whisky to deaden the pain those crippling injuries were causing. The suggestion was officially denied by club and player, but the legend stuck and whether true or not, the story wasn't dismissed as an outlandish fantasy. It typified the reputation he had managed to garner. As impressive as the second-half goals which totally overpowered Derby were, the team's run to the final saw them drawn away at every stage and need to overcome 5 replays – including 3 with Liverpool at the semi-final stage.

Beaten finalists after a replay in 1901, defeat came in part due to an error from the usually peerless Ernest Needham. United returned 12 months later to reclaim the cup.

All those games had been played at Crystal Palace but Old Trafford hosted the next final United contested, in 1915, in order not to disrupt travel in and around London during the advent of the First World War (see below).

There have been just 2 Cup final appearances at Wembley Stadium, in 1925 and 1936. The former was a match with Cardiff City and took on something of an international flavour. It was eventually decided by a single goal. So too was the encounter with Arsenal 11 years later. However, Bobby Barclay spurned a golden chance to snatch a goal for United in the opening minute; Alex Wilson dropped a cross at his feet but the winger could only push it straight back to the keeper. Jock Dodds struck the crossbar though blamed a push in the back from Wilf Copping for not being as accurate as he would normally have expected. Reaching the final possibly distracted United from grabbing promotion to the top flight that year. They finished in third place, 3 points off the runners-up spot after a very mixed run of results over the spring.

THE KHAKI CUP

War with Germany had been declared late in 1914 and the Football League was expected to be suspended at the close of that season. Chelsea were the opposition in what became known as the 'Khaki Cup', given that the crowd was mostly made up of uniformed soldiers. In truth the 3–0 scoreline in favour of the Blades was not as comprehensive as it sounded and had it not been for Stanley Fazackerly and Joseph Kitchen scoring within the last 7 minutes, Jimmy Simmons' single goal may well have decided the game. The suspension of all League and FA competitions meant the cup remained in the Bramall Lane trophy cabinet for the next 5 years. As a result, United retained the cup for the longest ever period of time. Another distinction about the game is that it was the first final initially played outside London. Manchester United's Old Trafford ground hosted the game as the authorities needed to restrict travel around the capital.

The Blades became the first and remain the only team to win the FA Cup during wartime.

FEW STARS OF TOMORROW

Youth internationals for the home nations have been quite rare at Bramall Lane. In fact until Phil Jagielka made a breakthrough in the early 2000s, England's Peter Beagrie was the only under-21 international to be recognised while at the club.

HAT-TRICKS

W. Robertson scored United's first-ever hat-trick in 1888, but Harry Hammond was the first to record a treble in the Football League and what's more in the club's first ever League game. Two players have managed to score hat-tricks in the same game on just a couple of occasions. Harry Johnson and Billy Mercer were the first in an 11–2 win over Cardiff City on 1 January 1926. The irrepressible Brian Deane and Tony Agana were the last duo to achieve this feat on 17 September 1988 in a 6–1 win over Chester City.

NATIONAL LEADERSHIP

The first United player to captain not just the club but the national side was revered by both fans and his peers. Although naturally a left-sided defender, Ernest Needham played in many other positions for the Blades and not just across the back line. His strength was probably his best attribute and allowed him to keep making robust challenges and surging runs with possession from the first whistle until the last. His brilliance and toughness in the tackle was renowned and he could often make opponents think twice about entering a duel with him. Affectionately nicknamed 'Nudger', he is still the only Blades skipper to lift the championship trophy. The title was the first honour in United's history, but 5 years earlier he had helped the club win promotion from Division Two. He also led his side to FA Cup glory in 1899 and 1902. Another title earned by Needham was 'The Prince of Half-Backs' – this was no idle boast either, as there were few players with better defensive qualities as demonstrated by the fact he was England's as well as United's first choice. Upon retiring at the grand old age of 37, he took up a scouting position at Bramall Lane.

AN EVER-PRESENT
ON THE TEAMSHEET

The sheer number of appearances made by Alan Woodward would suggest he spent a number of seasons as an ever-present in the line-up. He holds the club's record for the most uninterrupted seasons with 5. From 1968–71, 3 were consecutive. The other 2 were also back-to-back from 1973–5. The most number of players to ever negotiate a full league term without missing a game is also 5. This happened in the 1952/53 season when Burgin, Furniss, Shaw, Ringstead and Hawksworth played in all 42 games. Phew!

ONE-UP CLUB

Despite hundreds, in some cases many hundreds, of appearances for the Blades, a number of players have just one goal to show for all their efforts. Scoring certainly isn't the best way to gauge a contribution to the club, but still makes very interesting reading. Among the most notable members of this select club are Harry Latham who served United between 1946 and 1953. His only strike came during his second season in a Division One fixture at Stoke City's Victoria Ground. The game finished 1–1. Over the next 5 seasons of his United career, he failed to find the net.

The full list of 'one-up club' members who have played 50 league games or more follows:

Harry Latham	190
Peter Boyle	150
John Cutbush	126
Chris Wilder	99
Michael Whitham	86
David Barnes	82
Gary West	75
Colin Rawson	70
David Tuttle	63
Fred Hawley	57
Archie McPherson	57

To date only a couple of players have scored in their first and only appearance for United. J. Richardson was the first in September 1895 and may have expected at least one more chance after clinching a 2–1 win over Preston North End at Bramall Lane. The other member of this exclusive list is Stanley Taylor who also scored his one and only goal at home. The forward put the Blades 2–0 up against Notts County in a game United went on to win 3–1.

SEASON'S BEST SCORERS

The highest league scorer for a season in each division.

Premier League	Brian Deane	14	1992/93
Division One	Jimmy Dunne	41	1930/31
Division Two	Jock Dodds	34	1935/36
Division Three	Keith Edwards	33	1983/84
Division Four	Keith Edwards	35	1981/82

Only Arthur Brown has finished as the top flight's leading scorer while a Blade. His 22 goals in 1904/05 gained him that accolade. Jimmy Dunne may have expected his haul to have done the same in 1931, but he was beaten by Aston Villa's Tom Waring who grabbed a colossal 49 for the eventual runners-up.

MORE CLUBS
THAN TIGER WOODS?

It's often said that footballers like John Burridge are a dying breed, but the truth is there has never been anyone quite like the keeper known simply as 'Budgie'. Burridge is a man who, it is often quipped, had more clubs than Tiger Woods over the best part of 25 years and kept goal in 4 Premiership games well into his fifth decade. He made a debut in that competition in the 1994/95 season aged 43 years 4 months and 26 days, following an injury to Manchester City's Tony Coton. Burridge came on as a substitute in the game with Newcastle United – whom he was also serving as a goalkeeping coach at the time. Perhaps fittingly it finished goalless and possibly kept both his employers happy.

The man who could only be described as a veteran stopper played the last 3 games of the campaign. Two years on he finally retired though had been something of a 'gloves for hire' during most of his twilight seasons, playing no more than a handful of games for a host of sides offering experienced cover along with advice to youngsters.

One of the 15 professional clubs he turned out for was United, who acquired his services for just £10,000. At that stage he was just 3 months off his 33rd birthday – still in his prime. He immediately displaced Keith Waugh and his debut came in a 3–0 win over Wimbledon. Over the next 2½ years he helped United achieve mid-table finishes in Division Two. 3 years and 109 league appearances later he joined Southampton, earning the Blades a £20,000 profit. Burridge was involved in 33 transfers serving 27 clubs in total.

Just behind that tally is another former Blades keeper, Andy Dibble. The Welsh international who had 2 spells at Bramall Lane initially came to the club on loan from Manchester City in February 1997, then on a monthly contract at the beginning of the following campaign after he was released by the Maine Road outfit. He made no appearances but later in that campaign assisted Rangers to lift the Scottish Championship. The nature of his recruitment was indicative of Dibble's itinerant career which involved 18 clubs, 21 transfers and 8 loans. While playing for Barry Town, Dibble was hospitalised after suffering chemical burns when diving on pitch lines marked with hydrated lime.

CHAMPIONS OF ENGLAND

Like most clubs, Sheffield United have had their fair share of highs and lows – but are one of just 23 clubs to have been crowned Champions of England. The Blades were the fifth team to top Division One and the first from Yorkshire. A city at the very centre of the footballing world finally boasted the nation's top club in 1898. Although formed many years after their neighbours The Wednesday, Sheffield's only other League team, United found themselves eclipsing their rivals within a decade of being established. The Blades led the table from New Year's Day onwards but had been top for most weeks prior to that. They had spent no more than 10 days out of pole position and that came in the season's opening 3 games. Finishing 5 points clear of Sunderland was a huge margin of advantage.

Just 12 months on the Blades won the FA Cup but narrowly avoided a fate no champions wish to suffer and missed relegation by 4 points. Allied to United relief was the vicarious pleasure of watching Wednesday failing to beat the drop.

CHAMPIONS OF BRITAIN

As Football League champions the Blades took on their Scottish counterparts Celtic for the unofficial championship of Great Britain in 1898 over 2 legs played home and away. United were crowned the first and, to date, only British Champions, courtesy of an aggregate victory. A 1–0 home win – with Ralph Gaudie the scorer in the opening leg at Bramall Lane – proved just as crucial as Jack Almond's last-minute equaliser in the return fixture a little over a month later. It tied the score at 1–1 on the day but 2–1 overall. Aside from a banquet at Cutler's Hall, the team received medals plus a £3 bonus.

FROM TOP TO BOTTOM

The Blades' demotion to Division Four when the 1980/81 season closed made them the last of 3 teams to win the title then land in the basement division. There may have been 93 years between the 2 events but it was still a sad demise and one that Huddersfield Town and Portsmouth had experienced only a handful of seasons earlier.

THINKING ON THE SPOT

Charles Howett became the first United goalie to save a penalty. Joe Lievesley and Tom McAlister have both saved spot-kicks during league games, but only Alan Kelly has managed to stop 3 in a single match, albeit during a shoot-out with Coventry City in the sixth round of the 1997/98 FA Cup.

Harold Pantling, who was usually pressed into service as an emergency keeper, took the role when Harry Gough came off with 15 minutes to go in the first league game of the 1923/24 term. His call came when Gough was unable to continue after giving away a penalty kick. Pantling managed to make a fine save, quite literally with his first touch.

SHOOT-OUT SETBACKS

Until the close of the 2009/10 season Sheffield United had been involved in ten penalty shoot-outs, winning precisely half. The first of these tie-breaking mechanisms saw the Blades lose the Watney Mann Invitation Cup at Bristol Rovers' Eastville Stadium. No extra-time was played in the competition.

Three of the ten occasions in which Sheffield United have taken part in shoot-outs came in the 2004/05 season. Though United came through one of these, they exited the domestic cups after an additional 30 minutes failed to bring a result in the 2 other matches.

Here's a list of shoot-outs the Blades have participated in:

5 August 1972	Bristol Rovers	Watney Mann Invitation Cup	lost 7–6
22 October 1991	Notts County	Full Members Cup 2nd round	lost 2–1
16 March 1993	Blackburn Rovers	FA Cup 6th round replay	won 5–3
17 March 1998	Coventry City	FA Cup 6th round replay	won 3–1
21 December 1999	Rushden & Diamonds	FA Cup 3rd round replay	won 6–5
11 September 2001	Grimsby Town	League Cup 2nd round	lost 4–2
26 October 2004	Watford	League Cup 3rd round	lost 4–2
13 February 2005	West Ham United	FA Cup 4th round replay	won 3–1
1 March 2005	Arsenal	FA Cup 5th round replay	lost 4–2
20 September 2005	Shrewsbury Town	League Cup 2nd round	won 4–3

A GOOD DAY FOR THE KEEPER

Special attention is usually heaped on those players who make a goalscoring impact during their first games, but there have been 3 notable events at the other end of the field, including penalty saves on debut from Willie Foulke, Paul Tomlinson and Mervyn Day. Day's save actually came in his only appearance for the club, against Wimbledon on the final day of the 1991/92 season. A goalkeeping crisis forced the veteran custodian into action. The only keeper to have kept a penalty out during his league as well as United debut is Andy Leaning.

NULL AND VOID

Just 2 games involving the Blades have seen the results voided by the Football Association. The first was in 1890 when Burton Swifts beat United 2–1. However, it later came to light that Swifts had fielded an ineligible player. As a consequence the game was awarded to United. The other was almost 90 years later in an FA Cup tie with Arsenal – again lost by the odd goal in three. A late effort was scored after Nwankwo Kanu took a Ray Parlour throw then charged down the flank to cross for Marc Overmars to convert. Play had been restarted after Lee Morris received treatment for cramp, the ball having been put out for the injury to be tended. United were not expecting an attack and therefore were out of position. Blades fans were up in arms, especially as a seemingly clear-cut penalty had been denied earlier in the match. Steve Bruce called his players from the field. A rematch called due to the unsporting manner the goal was scored in also finished 2–1. Arsène Wenger initially made the suggestion and the FA concurred. However, as no laws had been broken and the result was valid, FIFA insisted that both sides sign declarations that the winner of a restaged game would progress.

WARNOCK'S RIFTS WITH REFS

Mere mention of Graham Poll's name is likely to see Neil Warnock's blood pressure surge. The former United boss, who is a qualified referee, entered a very public war of words with the official over that controversial 2003 FA Cup semi-final defeat saying: 'I shouldn't really say what I feel, but Poll was their best midfielder in the goal. I thought there was a foul before the goal, but they are given at one end and not the other.'

Though acknowledged as a good manager throughout the profession, Warnock is perhaps best termed as a 'Marmite figure' – loved and loathed in equal measure. Other referees to incur his wrath include David Elleray, Richard Beeby, Jim Rushton, Trevor Massey and Rob Shoebridge. There have been many more along the way, added to run-ins with players, fans, directors and his peers over a managerial career stretching almost 3 decades. None of these disputes have been confined to opponents. Even those among his own number have realised there is no discrimination in targets.

A FIRST MILLENNIUM

The Blades became only the fifth club to amass an aggregate of 1,000 points by virtue of beating Newcastle United at Bramall Lane on 15 September 1923. 1,000 league games were put under the club's belt during the same 1923/24 season – the final game at West Bromwich Albion bringing up that landmark.

PICTURES OF THE BLADES

Football and the movies haven't always sat easily together. Very few films centred around the game have proved successful, despite the popularity of the 2 pastimes and the action scenes often look wholly unconvincing. *Escape to Victory* is cited as a notable exception by some. Fewer have that feeling about *When Saturday Comes* which hit cinemas in 1996. It profiles the rise of a brewery worker and pub player, Jimmy Muir, portrayed by Blades fan and former Bramall Lane board member Sean Bean. Muir eventually pulls a Sheffield United shirt on despite coming to the game late in life and battling against a drink problem. There may be some who have yet to see the finished production – even many years since its release – so there will be no spoilers. Suffice to say, in no small part due to Muir's exploits, United do quite well in the FA Cup. Former Blade Tony Currie also stars as himself.

An even wider audience became aware of the Blades thanks to the success of *The Full Monty*. Robert Carlyle wore a United shirt throughout most of the film and along with his co-stars often made mention of the team. *Batman Begins* also features a small boy in a United top handing some fruit to Bruce Wayne played by Christian Bale. Whether it was enough to justify the establishment of a Hollywood Blades Supporters' Club is another matter. A former Blade to have acquitted himself in the world of films is of course Vinnie Jones who has managed to build himself an acting career on the back of featuring in *Lock, Stock and Two Smoking Barrels*. Since then the former midfielder has appeared in a number of other movies including big-budget offerings.

Though he claims to watch for the results of both Sheffield United and Wednesday, Michael Palin, born and raised in the city's Broomhill district, is a boyhood Blade. Inspiration for the 'Golden

Gordon' character in *Ripping Yarns* and his fury at the plight of Barnstoneworth United is not specifically based around Sheffield United's travails. While some disappointments as a spectator played their part, allusions to the decline of Huddersfield Town were more appropriate at the time of filming.

ONE-TIME BLADES

Of those to have played just once for Sheffield United, Chris Bettney, Martin Dickinson, Carl Muggleton, Nathan Peel, Nigel Steane and Paul Wood made their bows as substitutes. One famous name who also made just one appearance was Ernest Needham, although not the same one most United fans fondly refer to as the 'Prince of Half-Backs'. This particular Ernest Needham was also a defender, but played during November 1912 in a 2–0 win over Notts County 2 seasons after his namesake had retired.

QUICK OFF THE MARK

The scant nature of football's early record books makes giving the answer as to who has notched United's fastest goal a difficult one to verify. However, the fastest recorded strike by a Blades player came after 8 seconds when Ron Simpson put the ball through Burnley's net on 26 October 1963. The quickest goal ever scored in the Blades favour is said to have come after just 3 seconds when Swansea Town's Sid Lawrence scored an own goal in the league match played on 13 November 1937. The goal set United on the way to a 5–3 win. The quickest debutante goalscorer is Danny Webber – against Leeds United, 93 seconds into the loan spell that preceded his permanent move to Bramall

Lane in April 2005. That shaded the mark set by John Blair who scored 2 minutes into a game with Cardiff City on 26 November 1927.

A LOT OF GOOD WORK
FOR CHARITY

United played in the first ever Charity Shield match in March 1898 against Corinthians. The Mayor of London's Charity Shield, as it was then known, eventually ended up being shared after the first match and then a replay were drawn. United refused to play extra-time in protest at some of the refereeing decisions made during the 2 matches.

FAMILIARITY BREEDS CONTENT

Consistency is usually a byword for success. The Blades were able to play the same goalkeeper, defenders and centre forward for the initial 21 games of the 1958/59 campaign. They lost 7 and won 9 of those fixtures.

THE HARDMAN'S HARDMAN

A number of tough players are labelled footballing hardmen, but all those regarded as such around the 1980s and 1990s note striker Billy Whitehurst as the toughest of them all. He frightened even the most comfortable-looking and daunting defenders; even his own team-mates found him terrifying. The lower ranks of the South Yorkshire scene provided a steep learning curve, as did his first steps in the professional game. A nomadic career was said to be supplemented by income from bare-knuckle fights during his time with Oxford United. The Blades were Billy's seventh club and his stay lasted just over a year with later stops in Northern Ireland, Australia, Hong Kong and China plus all levels of the domestic game.

FRIENDS ACROSS THE SEAS

Many English clubs decide to create alliances with teams from other leagues, the idea being that both parties would benefit. The smaller outfit gets a loan of rising stars who strengthen their line-ups and the bigger team buy their youngsters valuable first-team experience. United opened negotiations about this type of deal with Scottish League Division One side Inverness Caledonian Thistle in August 2000. The club has since forged alliances with various nations and have played on every continent, including extensive tours of South America, Australasia, northern and southern Africa, North America and even the Caribbean.

The most fervent links are to China and Hungary. In January 2006 United became owners of Chinese club Chengdu Wunju who subsequently became known as the Chengdu Blades. It opened up a lucrative market in that increasingly affluent country and a friendly to mark the deal was very well attended. Fittingly it ended 1–1. A fair number of Chengdu shirts can also be seen around the city of Sheffield. Petr Katchouro and Li Tie have played for both sides.

Just over 2 years later Hungarian outfit Ferencváros were purchased too. Land around the stadium was also developed and the Budapest side were managed by former centre-back Craig Short until the summer of 2010 who succeeded ex-Blades player and coach Bobby Davison. Short had taken a sabbatical from the Lake District boating company he co-owns. On the playing side, those to have plied their trade in Hungary include James Ashmore, Justin Haber, Paul Shaw and Rafe Wolfe. Somalian international Liban Abdi has spent an extensive loan in Budapest but was released at the close of the 2009/10 season.

Crack Brazilian outfit and 2005 World Champions São Paulo, Australian A-League club Central Coast Mariners and Belgium side White Star Woluwe enjoy strategic development programmes with Sheffield United. Rafe Wolfe has not only been a registered professional with the United and Ferencváros but also White Star. Other than the loan of Keith Quinn, a skipper of various youth teams and the reserves to the Mariners, the South American and Aussie partnerships have yet to bear a share of players above academy grade. A strange facet of Quinn's time down under was that the Australian League was in its off-season for much of the time he spent there. São Paulo have taken part in junior tournaments at Bramall Lane, one visitor to the 2007 competition being the man whose name was attached to the trophy contested for – Pelé.

ISLAND-HOPPING

United have played on virtually each major island dotted around the British coast and along with Sheffield Wednesday became the first professional outfit to journey half way across the Irish Sea to the Isle of Man for a game in May 1948. Honours finished even at 2–2.

GIVE IT SOME HEAT

Under-soil heating was installed at Bramall Lane in the 1980s but not needed until the 1995/96 season when a game against Millwall was threatened by icy weather. The only problem was that someone forgot to turn it on and the threatened match had to be cancelled.

THE BATTLE OF BRAMALL LANE

The Blades have been involved in some of the heaviest sending-off incidents of recent times, including the so-called Battle of Bramall Lane towards the end of the 2001/02 season. The dismissals of Simon Tracy, Georges Santos and Patrick Suffo are among the most notorious in the history of the domestic game and caused an abandonment in circumstances without precedent.

Tensions were high in the stands between the two sets of supporters when United entertained West Bromwich Albion on 16 March and just 8 minutes into the game, keeper Tracey was sent off for a deliberate handball outside his area.

With the exception of run-of-the-mill fouls, the first half went ahead without much incident. But, soon after the restart, Michael Brown was booked for a foul. 3 minutes later Santos and Suffo were sent on as substitutes. In his first involvement Santos made a two-footed tackle on Andy Johnson who fortunately managed to evade the worst possible effects of the challenge but was still left prone. Almost exactly a year to the day earlier, Johnson, then of Nottingham Forest, collided with Santos, his arm connecting to the Frenchman's face. Five hours of surgery were required while a titanium plate was inserted in his shattered cheekbone.

Players from both sides rushed to the incident and a mass brawl ensued. During the mêlée Suffo, who had already been in hot water in France after physically attacking an official, head-butted Derek McInnes no more than a few yards away from the referee. He also received a red card and had to be led from the pitch. No more than 10 minutes later Keith Curle became the final player to enter the book.

United were forced to withdraw Brown and Robert Ullathorne through injury, leaving just 6 players on the field and referee Eddie Wolstenholme had no choice but to abandon the game 82 minutes in with West Brom leading 3–0. Brown limping off met with muted accusations of feigned injury – though it is worth noting the midfielder missed the next couple of games. Conjecture about the possible consequences hung over the club for a number of days as did the range of decisions about the result, but first steps in resolving the issue came when the Football League awarded Albion the 3 points they would probably have earned. United later received a £10,000 fine.

Bad blood was nothing new in the history of the fixture. When the sides met at The Hawthorns a season earlier, manager Neil Warnock had to be restrained at the final whistle as a result of his anger at Robert Ullathorne's sending off for a challenge on Lee Hughes who scored a winning goal.

ANOTHER QUARTET OFF

The Blades have been involved in one of the few occasions 4 players have been dismissed in a match – a Second Division clash with Portsmouth on 13 December 1986. Then in 1994 during an Anglo-Italian cup match with Udinese, 3 players were shown the red card along with manager Dave Bassett following a heated exchange with the officials. The Italians also had a player sent off as part of the same incident which riled Bassett so much.

QUICKLY INTO THE BOOK

Vinnie Jones has the quickest ever booking in league football, though not while a United player. That early yellow came while in the blue of Chelsea against the Blades little more than a year after leaving Bramall Lane. Just 3 seconds after kick-off he clattered into Dane Whitehouse to earn a caution. That beat his previous record of 5 seconds earned in red and white stripes when clashing with Manchester City's Peter Reid in similar circumstances. The warning which accompanied the card went unheeded – 55 minutes in he was booked for another foul on his fellow midfielder. That's just 1 of 12 career dismissals.

Chris Morgan is United's most dismissed player with 6 red cards brandished in almost 300 games. A dismissal against Hull City towards the end of the 2007/08 season was his last to date, though he has attracted 15 yellow cards in the two seasons since. That brings his total cautions above 50 over 7 seasons.

Although this course of action would not be allowed in a first-class game, Bob Cain managed to avert an early bath when he was sent off in a friendly against Arsenal in October 1892 by apologising. The expression of regret accepted, he was invited back on to the field to see out the remainder of the game.

NO NEIGHBOURLY LOVE

On 18 February 1900 perhaps the most ill-tempered Steel City derby took place. Added to the couple of dismissals suffered, Sheffield Wednesday's George Lee was forced to leave the fray after breaking a leg in a challenge for the ball and in retaliation the Owls players decided to kick back – literally. Ambrose Langley was dismissed for a badly executed tackle on Walter Bennett but had already forced the referee to warn him after conceding a penalty minutes after the restart. Ernest Needham scored from the resulting spot-kick. John Pryce joined Langley in an early bath when he lashed out at George Hedley.

GONE IN
ZERO SECONDS

Keith Gillespie is one of just two players in the entire history of the game to be dismissed before he had played a single second of a match. At least in a technical sense – as he was on the pitch, kitted out and the game had already commenced. During the Premier League meeting with Reading in January 2007 he had just come on the field as a substitute replacing Derek Geary. However, before the referee could blow his whistle to restart play he saw Gillespie elbow Stephen Hunt square in the jaw and inevitably waved a red card in his direction. His time on the field was measured at 12 seconds. As he left the pitch, Gillespie pushed Hunt in the face. For the record Walter Boyd is the only other man to achieve the feat: he did so 7 years before the Northern Irish international as an employee of Swansea City.

There was a fair degree of antipathy between Gillespie and Reading. The winger was lucky not to have been sent off after an incident against the same opposition in a league game at the Madejski Stadium. A fairly blatant penalty had been denied for a foul 10 minutes from time and Gillespie, who had been body checked and then watched Brynjar Gunnarsson score with a minute remaining, had words with the official. Referees can of course exert their authority after the final whistle, but faced with the player and manager Neil Warnock, Grant Hegley who had overlooked Paddy Kenny's handball outside the area earlier in the game, merely looked to make an exit. Maybe he didn't like dishing out red cards. It certainly seems Gillespie's analysis should have earned some sanction for dissent but the official opted not to issue one leading to a charge of failing to apply the laws of the game properly. Warnock was punished by the FA for his part. 24 days later the pair met again in a Carling Cup tie at the same venue. Gillespie was one of many first-team players rested for the encounter.

On another occasion goalkeeper Paddy Kenny was dismissed for an altercation in the players' tunnel with Millwall skipper Kevin Muscat at half-time. Their feud was spotted by a fourth official rather than the referee or his assistants. It meant Phil Jagielka had to take a turn between the posts. The central defender did well in the 2–1 win, though was beaten once. It was a shock for the fans who may have assumed there was an injury to the keeper until questioning why his deputy hadn't been called upon and why each side were reduced to 10 men.

THE COCA-COLA KID

When Brighton & Hove Albion sold Colin Kazim Richards (as he was then known) to Sheffield United for £150,000 it may have seemed like a piece of poor business given that the forward had cost them £250,000 when purchased from Bury just a year earlier. However, to be more precise Richards was bought by Seagulls fan Aaron Berry who had been armed with a quarter of a million pounds by Coca-Cola to promote their sponsorship of the Football League. Brighton, rather than Berry, took the transfer fee once Richards departed the South Coast. Unfortunately things never really happened for Richards at Bramall Lane and after a single season he joined Fenerbahce for an estimated £1.2 million. Despite a few setbacks in Istanbul, Kâzim-Kâzim Richards (as he is now known) has played in the Champions League and represented Turkey.

A DOUBLE CENTURY

Not a time-based or even cricket reference, but a nod to the number of seasons United have conceded or scored 100 league goals or more. To date each distinction has only been achieved once but the 1929/30 campaign almost finished with 100 goals under each heading. The Blades finished 20th and just 1 place above relegation to Division Two after hitting the target 91 times but conceding a huge 96 goals. Only 3 teams hit more goals – including champions Sheffield Wednesday. But just 1 side had an even worse 'goals against' column – Burnley who finished level on points but as a result of that excellent record at the other end trailed by 0.14 on goal average and took the drop.

United's players managed to tally 102 goals from the 42 games played over the 1925/26 term and conceded 101 during the poor run suffered over the 1933/34 season when the Blades finished rock-bottom. That record-breaking 1925/26 campaign featured an 11–2 win over Cardiff City. A few weeks earlier Manchester City were hammered 8–3, then 7 days later the

Blades beat City 4–1 at Maine Road. Burnley were beaten 6–1 towards the end of the season.

WITH A LITTLE HELP FROM THE REF

Gareth Taylor scored a couple in United's 2–1 win over Bradford City on 28 February 1998 but enjoyed a slice of luck with the game's opener just past the half-hour mark. Eddie Youds made a punt upfield but only found the head of referee Roger Furnandiz, after which the ball cannoned 25 yards in the wrong direction. Taylor took it on his chest then coolly despatched beyond the keeper. The Doncaster official looked apologetic but had to award the goal.

However, Tring's Graham Poll did the Blades no favours in the 2003 FA Cup semi-final at Old Trafford against Arsenal. During the build-up to Freddie Ljungberg's deciding goal he accidentally collided with Michael Tonge meaning there was one less man able to thwart the Gunners. There was no offer of a replay this time from Arsène Wenger who had seen his team pushed hard. In part their lead only survived due to David Seaman's reflexes.

BALLOONED UNDER THE BAR

Luton Shelton made the most of a tendency Manchester City fans once had to throw blue and white balloons onto the pitch just before kick-off. A dozen minutes had passed in an FA Cup fourth round tie with the Blues in February 2008, meaning many of the objects had yet to be popped by City keeper Joe Hart, his defenders or the stewards. There were a huge number in the six-yard box when Lee Martin sent in a low centre. The ball reared up off one of the stray balloons and caused Michael Ball to air-kick. Shelton toe-poked the ball in from a few yards.

DUAL NATIONALITY

FIFA outlawed the practice of internationals 'changing allegiances' in 1960. Even though it wasn't an easy thing to do, in the governing bodies' eyes far too many professionals were adopting new countries in order to win caps. It is now only allowed in certain circumstances and of course should a once-established nation split into 2 or more parts – as has happened throughout Europe since the early 1990s. Irish players were legitimately allowed to switch between the North and Republic before 1950.

United's Bob Evans became one of the few players to have turned out for 2 different countries by virtue of being born in Chester, a city which straddles both sides of the English/Welsh border. Both his parents were Welsh and such heritage gave that nation their dib on call-ups. But by virtue of his birthplace being revealed to the FA, they awarded him an England cap against Scotland in 1911. He had already made 10 appearances for Wales, 4 of which were during his time at Bramall Lane and all against England.

Former Blade Barry Hayles was one of many players called up by the Cayman Islands for vital World Cup qualifiers with Cuba in 2000. The Caribbean nation, which remains a British overseas dependency, believed they had identified a loophole in the rules and could bring in UK passport holders. Hayles and 6 other English-based players turned out in a warm-up tie with USA outfit DC United, but FIFA were quick to quash the hopes of a full cap insisting that residency, birth and family heritage were the only criteria for eligibility. It was via the latter that Hayles played for Jamaica – making his debut against Cuba.

David Johnson, who had a month's loan at Bramall Lane, played for England B and came close to making Glenn Hoddle's senior side in 1998. He eventually played for Jamaica (he was born in the capital city Kingston), but had been heavily courted by Wales and had actually agreed to turn out for Scotland before it was found he didn't meet the necessary criteria. Joshua Sloan, better known as Paddy, was one of many Irish-born players to turn out for the national sides north and south of the Irish border immediately after the war. As a club player he also took to the field in 5 separate countries – along with his nation of birth, there was England, Italy, Malta and Australia.

HOME INTERNATIONALS

During the early 1900s United had a massive compliment of fully-capped internationals. At one time there were no fewer than a dozen on the books. To date 73 internationals have turned out for their respective countries – 34 wore England jerseys during their time at Bramall Lane and Ernest Needham is the most capped with 16 appearances. The first were Harry Liley and Mick Whitham who made their debuts on the same day and at the same time – but in different games. As they had done on two previous occasions, the FA picked 2 teams to play matches simultaneously. Selection was based on which players had amateur or professional status. The former, including Liley, played Wales at the Racecourse Ground, Wrexham. Those who turned out for pay, such as Whitham, met Ireland at the delightfully named Solitude – the Belfast home of Cliftonville.

Billy Gillespie is the most capped player in the club's history with 25 Northern Ireland outings earned during his time with the Blades.

BLADES GREATS NOT GOOD ENOUGH FOR ENGLAND

Len Badger played for England schools, all manner of national youth sides as an older teenager then the under-23s and the Football League. However, he is widely accepted as one of the best players and almost certainly the finest right-back never to have won a senior cap. Keith Newton and George Cohen stood in his way. The same was true for winger Alan Woodward. The outside-right failed to gain anything other than the odd outing at youth grade, though all too often his hot head was seen as a bar to gaining the ultimate accolade. No matter to the Blades. Between them both men racked up well over 1,000 appearances for Sheffield United.

FROM FOREIGN FIELDS

The cosmopolitan nature of the modern game ensures that players born far from the city of Sheffield have turned out for the club. Up until the close of the 2009/10 season, various countries outside the home nations had been represented by Blades. They are:

Carl Veart, Shaun Murphy and Duggie Hodgson (Austrialia)
Paul Ifill (Barbados)
Petr Katchouro (Belarus)
Patrick Suffo (Cameroon)
Li Tie (China)
Paul Peschisolido (Canada)
Ahmed Fathi (Egypt)

Mihkel Aksalu (Estonia)

Vas Borbokis (Greece)

Oliver Tebily (Ivory Coast)

Luton Shelton (Jamaica)

Jostein Flo and Roger Nilsen (Norway)

Jimmy Dunne, Alan Kelly, Alf Ringstead, Paddy Kenny and Alan
   Quinn (Republic of Ireland)

Peter Ndlovu (Zimbabwe)

FAMOUS NAMES, FAMOUS PLACES

Over the course of 121 years some people with familiar-sounding names outside the game have turned out for United. Eddie Grant, Mick Jones, Shaun Murphy, Bernard Shaw and Mick Hill provide namesakes from the worlds of art, music, sport and literature. There is a 'close but no cigar' for Barry Butlin. As for famous places they are replicated in the shape of major cities and countries in the surnames of Andy Barnsley, Joe Bolton, Dave Bradford, Gary Brazil, Alan Cork, Shaun Derry, Gary France, Paul Holland, Stewart Houston, Terry Poole, Neil Ramsbottom, Stan Rhodes and Trevor Ross. 'Chico', Des, Ian and William share the Hamilton family name.

Although plenty of players share surnames with various parts of Yorkshire, districts of the city of Sheffield are more sparse in their representation with just Curtis Woodhouse.

WORLD CUP BLADES

Just 6 Sheffield United players have been selected for World Cup duty while on the club's books. The first was Ted Burgin, a non-playing goalkeeper and deputy to Birmingham City's Gil Merrick for the 1954 finals. The full list is as follows:

Ted Burgin	England	1954
Alan Hodgkinson	England	1958 and 1962
Jostein Flo	Norway	1994
Roger Nilsen	Norway	1994
Alan Kelly	Republic of Ireland	1994
Patrick Suffo	Cameroon	2002

IT COULD HAVE BEEN BRAMALL LANE RATHER THAN THE NOU CAMP

The signing of Alejandro or Alex Sabella would not have marked the first time an Argentinian had pulled on a United shirt had the club's board decided they couldn't take a £200,000 punt on a youth international called Diego Maradona. Especially as additional fees and payments would almost double that amount over the course of a contract. Prior to narrowly missing out on a place in the 1978 World Cup staged in his homeland, the 17-year-old Maradona had been scouted on a trip to South America by manager Harry Haslam. The player was happy to sign up and agreed a deal but was forced to remain with Argentinos Juniors, then eventually play for Barcelona and Napoli among others. Sabella, a more known quantity at that stage, cost £40,000 less, though was something of a curio in the Second Division, then the third tier. His final outing was in a County Cup final with Sheffield Wednesday. He signed off with a goal and a winners' medal. Part of the deal was a challenge match with Sabella's old club, River Plate. They had rarely travelled to Europe at that time and had never visited England before but won 2–1. 22,244 fans watched the game.

When Juan Sebastián Verón was reported to have stated that his boyhood dream had been to play for Sheffield United rather than Manchester United not long after signing up at Old Trafford for £28.1 million, many thought the comment was a joke. However, the midfielder became something of a long-distance Blade due to his uncle, Pedro Verde, turning out for the club between 1978 and 1981. Prior to that Verde was a team-mate of Verón's father at Estudiantes. Unfortunately Verde, another recruit for Harry Haslam, didn't have the best spell of his career at the Lane making just 10 appearances in his first season before being relegated to the reserves for a couple of years. There was always a feeling he was brought over to provide Sabella with a familiar face and someone to talk to. When conflict in the Falkland Islands loomed large, his contract was cancelled to ensure he experienced no bad feeling. That said he was believed by some to have left with a plundered souvenir – the Yorkshire and Humberside Cup – which disappeared after his final game and has never been seen since.

LOAN STARS

Clubs often sign players on loan to provide experienced cover for various positions or to allow other clubs' charges to gain essential first-team experience. The system is criticised with many believing it has been overused, if not abused, in recent times. It has certainly led to a high player turnover among Premier and Football League clubs. All too often those introduced add little to their temporary employers. For players going out from Bramall Lane on a similar basis, Jordan Robertson is the most lent-out, having joined 7 clubs. A prolific scorer in the lower ranks, he has made just 2 substitute appearances in the League Cup and due to a prison sentence for dangerous driving late in 2009, may have to wait for a second chance. So far he has been farmed out to Torquay United, Northampton Town, Dundee United, Oldham Athletic, Southampton, Ferencváros and Bury.

PLAYED IN THE USA

United have signed and subsequently seen a number of players turn out in the USA after leaving the club. Indoor and outdoor football have, at times, been popular in a country which has resisted the beautiful game more earnestly than any other. Though previously viewed as a college or youth sport, there have been many guises. All on the list below have appeared in either the North American Soccer League (NASL), American Soccer League (ASL) or Major League Soccer (MLS), plus what is effectively the current structure's lower tiers in the United Soccer Leagues (USL).

David Bradford is the most traveled; brought across the Atlantic by his former Sheffield United boss Ken Furphy, he spent the final 6 years of his career in the States and after a lengthy spell as a postmaster in Blackburn, returned to coach children in Tulsa. Alan Woodward left the Lane in 1978 joining Tulsa Roughnecks. His deadly striking of the ball earned admirers across the spectrum of sports, including American Football, and he was offered the role of specialist goal-kicker with the

Oklahoma Thunder. He played no part in the game other than taking a strike at the uprights for field goals or converting touchdowns. The sport's rules allowed his rolling substitution on and off the field when a kick was awarded.

Peter Anderson	San Diego Sockers and Tampa Bay Rowdies
Jeff Bourne	Dallas Tornado and Atlanta Chiefs
Dave Bradford	Detroit Express, Washington Diplomats, Tulsa Roughnecks, Baltimore Blast, Seattle Sounders
Jim Brown	Detroit Express, Washington Diplomats and Chicago Sting
Cliff Calvert	Toronto Blizzard, Dallas Tornado and Buffalo Stallions (indoor)
Bobby Campbell	Vancouver Whitecaps
Franz Carr	Pittsburgh Riverhounds
Eddie Colquhoun	Detroit Express and Washington Diplomats
Tony Currie	Toronto Nationals
John Cutbush	Wichita Wings
Keith Eddy	New York Cosmos
Tony Field	New York Cosmos
Colin Franks	Toronto Blizzard
Terry Garbett	New York Cosmos
Ian 'Chico' Hamilton	Minnesota Kicks
Trevor Hockey	San Diego Jaws, Las Vegas Quicksilvers and San José Earthquakes
David Irving	Fort Lauderdale Strikers, Tulsa Roughnecks, Atlanta Chiefs and San José Earthquakes
Nicky Johns	Tampa Bay Rowdies

Jimmy Johnstone	San José Earthquakes
John McGeady	South California Lasers
Terry Phelan	Charleston Battery
John Ryan	Seattle Sounders
Alan Woodward	Tulsa Roughnecks and Memphis Rouges

THREE TIMES A CHARM

The player to have most permanent spells with United is Brian Deane, who among 9 professional clubs, had 3 stints at Bramall Lane and 2 with Leeds United. An initial 5-year stay was ended by a switch to Elland Road. It took almost £3 million to take the forward away and £1.5 million to land him back 4 seasons later, though the second spell only lasted 5½ months before the chance to play for Benfica presented itself. There was another turn lasting just less than half a year at the close of the then 38-year-old veteran's career. Two substitute appearances brought his number of appearances across all competitions to 271. An impressive tally of 120 goals were scored from those outings.

Leigh Bromby has also had 3 stints with the Blades though 1 of these came on loan from Watford. He initially signed on a free transfer from Sheffield Wednesday and became one of just a handful of players to make a century of appearances for each of the city's clubs before joining the Hertfordshire-based outfit in a deal which could rise to £850,000. His last appearance as a Blade was against the Hornets who, a year into his tenure, granted a 6-month return to Bramall Lane with the promise of a permanent deal. Though a 2-year contract was penned just 8 weeks in, after a sole League Cup appearance, he was allowed to join Leeds United's push to make it out of League One. As a boy in Dewsbury he had supported the Whites, who he saw lift the league title as an 11-year-old. Jon Harley has enjoyed 2 loan spells at Bramall Lane while a Fulham player, and a year-long permanent period as a Blade.

ONE OF THE LEAGUE'S BEST

Up to the close of the 2009/10 season, United had spent 97 seasons in the Football League playing 3,948 games and winning 1,568 ties; 966 have been drawn and 1,414 lost. In the process of this, United have scored 6,177 goals and conceded 5,850. Their total points tally over this time is a huge 4,430. United are currently the twelfth most successful Football League team ever in terms of this last criterion. Up to the close of the 2009/10 season 132 Premiership points have been amassed from 122 games.

AN END OF SEASON PARTY

While most teams completed their 1946/47 season on 7 June, the Blades were forced to continue for a while longer. It was the first proper League campaign staged after the Second World War and originally had a scheduled completion date of 26 April. This had to be scrapped when Government regulations banned previously postponed matches from being rearranged during midweek. This situation was further aggravated by the weather, meaning that United were forced to wait an extra week before concluding their campaign against Stoke City. The Blades did at least round off the season with a win. The visitors were beaten 2–1. No team has ever finished a Football League season later than this. As the next season began on 23 August, there were

just a few days more than a 10-week break before competitive
football started again.

LEAGUE CUP LOYALTY

While other teams shunned the League Cup during its debut
season and subsequent campaigns, the Blades have proved one
of its greatest supporters, having never missed a season. Despite
this loyalty United had never progressed beyond the last eight (in
1961/62, 1966/67 and 1971/72), before reaching the semi-final
of the 2002/03 competition. Liverpool went through by the odd
goal in 5 over 2 hard-fought legs. The club's first match in the
competition against Bury ended in a 3–1 defeat when Joe Nibloe
became the first Blade to score a League Cup goal after roughly a
minute of the game.

GOALSCORING GOALKEEPERS

Over the years 3 United keepers have managed to find the
opposition's net, although it should be noted that these strikes
were all in friendlies. The first was Willie Foulke in a game with
Kaffirs on 23 October 1899. Not to be outdone in any area of
the game, Foulke bagged another in a 7–2 win. That was the
only occasion the keeper was actually playing in goal. Both Paul
Tomlinson and John Burridge made marks as outfield players
when they found themselves on the score sheet – Tomlinson
against the Dallas Americans on 31 May 1985 when he wrapped
up a 2–0 win. Burridge actually notched a brace in the 9–1 win
over a Guernsey XI on 12 May 1986.

TAKING A TURN BETWEEN THE POSTS

At one time, when a deputy was sought from the outfield to cover for an injured goalkeeper, Albert Sturgess – known as the one-man football team due to his prowess across many areas of the field – was the popular choice during the majority of his career. It is estimated he played somewhere in the region of 330 minutes in goal, during which time he conceded 8 strikes. Alan Woodward was the main man throughout much of the 1960s and '70s when specialist custodians were unable to continue. A leader of the club's scoring charts at the end of the season on 7 occasions, he also performed wonders at the other end of the pitch. During one match in 1967 he played the vast majority of a game – 80 minutes – against Leeds United as an emergency keeper. Though busy, he was most importantly an unbeaten stand-in. John Pemberton took over from Simon Tracey on his league debut for the Blades. Tracey had fractured a cheekbone in the first game of the season after an accidental collision with Liverpool's Ian Rush. The full-back took over in goal after just 15 minutes and gave a creditable performance even though the then league champions won 3–1.

When Everton needed to change their custodian during a league game in February 1895, the Blades strikers faced no fewer than 3 keepers. The Merseysiders were 2–0 up within the opening quarter of an hour. Soon afterwards Dick Williams had to be relieved of his duties. Bob Kelso replaced him – a strange choice considering he was nursing a hand injury. Before the break Harry Hammond had levelled matters. Kelso was clearly struggling so Alf Milward took over until the close. He was powerless to stop Hammond grabbing a treble and then John Docherty making it 4–2.

Striker Colin Collindridge was used to great effect during a game with Manchester United in January 1948 when Jack Smith was injured with 83 minutes remaining. The Red Devils grabbed a lead before Collindridge had time to acclimatise to his role, and soon after Ernest Jackson missed a penalty. However, a couple of George Jones strikes and a solid display from the stand-in stopper set up an enthralling and unlikely 2–1 victory.

HIGH-SCORING FRIENDLIES

There have been a number of high-scoring friendly games but United have scored 10 goals or more just 3 times. 11–1 was the scoreline against Skegness Town in August 1986; 12–1 v a Hagfors XI from Sweden in July 1988 and 10–0 when playing Ljusne GAIK, again of Sweden, in July 1992.

UNITED
AGAINST THE WORLD

An early meeting with a country's national team came with a visit to Tel Aviv in February 1972 to play Israel. The club also trekked to Brunei for a match against the Israeli national side in September 1983 to celebrate their new national stadium being opened. The Blades won 1–0 and the next day earned a 1–1 draw against a Brunei invitational team.

LEAGUE HOPES IN ASHES

After serving in the Midland Counties then Northern Leagues, United's first application to join the Football League was technically unsuccessful even if the Blades were accepted to the take part in the newly formed Second Division. The initial bid came as a result of the powers that be announcing an intention to expand its number from 14 to 16. Sheffield Wednesday also applied, but while the Owls were given immediate passage through – possibly due to claiming fourth place in the Football Alliance being perceived as a good achievement – United fell just 1 vote short at the count-up.

When a recount was requested, the League informed the Bramall Lane board that the papers had been burned. However, such was the clamour for places that another tier would be formed and United had been accepted for membership. As teams like Preston North End, Burnley, Woolwich Arsenal and indeed Wednesday would not be regular visitors to the Lane by virtue of this decision, it caused worries about the popularity of the new structure and whether sufficient money could be generated to ensure survival. It worried the club so much that the board decided that United would not resign their place in the Northern League. These misgivings were dispelled by promotion to the top flight at the first attempt.

GOING GREEN

George Green earned much acclaim as an amateur on the thriving non-league scene in Leamington. Though an excellent wing-half his versatility was put to the test through the assignment of many roles including jobs on either flank, deep or advanced positions. Although he stood at 5ft 9in he was nonetheless a powerfully built man who used this advantage well and rarely suffered injury as a result. However, there was one much talked about occasion when he suffered a dislocation of his shoulder in a match with Blackburn Rovers. United lost the game 7–5 but Green only came off the field to have the joint popped back into place without the protection of anaesthetic or other forms of pain-killer. He bravely played his usual robust game despite the discomfort. In front of goal he maintained a cool head and rarely missed any of the scoring chances he found himself presented with.

LET THERE BE LIGHT

The first floodlit game to be staged anywhere in the world took place at Bramall Lane on 14 October 1878. Members of various local teams formed the make-up of the Reds and Blues. Estimates say the number of spectators at the ground that night could have been as high as 20,000, but the official receipts stated that 12,000 people paid £300 in total to gain admission. Journalists recording events stated that many scaled the walls in order to view the match free of charge. Four lights were mounted on 30ft poles producing the equivalent light of 8,000 candles. As experiments go, it was a huge success. A commemorative coin was produced depicting the scene ahead of the Euro 96 Championships, but the purpose wasn't related to night-time football or any other sport. The lighting used was designed and intended to illuminate work sites of a similar range to a football pitch, so this game allowed a perfect illustration of its capabilities. The Blues ran out 2–0 winners.

Like most clubs United installed their first set of permanent floodlights during the 1950s. They were unveiled on 16 March 1954 before a specially arranged friendly with Rotherham United. 17,787 came through the turnstiles and a further 10 games were organised to get fans used to the innovation. Scottish and European clubs were among the other guests, though

Brazilians. Bela Vista were visitors in October 1958. Originally 4 pylons were erected with a fifth added prior to Bela Vista's arrival. Three years later their height was increased to measure a huge 145ft. They have undergone many changes since and even a complete replacement, in 1995, when the pylons were ditched in favour of lighting fastened to the stands.

BAD LIGHT STOPPED PLAY

The first United game to be abandoned was a friendly with Doncaster Rovers on 28 December 1889. Although those new-fangled floodlights had already been used at Bramall Lane like so many other grounds, Belle Vue had no such facilities and the players were forced off 10 minutes from the end when darkness dropped over the ground.

HOCKEY GROUNDED

Trevor Hockey was probably denied a longer career with Sheffield United than he or the club would have preferred by a broken leg towards the end of the 1971/72 season. The man considered something of a cult hero struggled to return from that setback and left almost a year to the day later in a swap for Norwich City's Jimmy Bone. Hockey became one of a handful of players to ply his trade on all 92 grounds used by League clubs during the 1970s. He also played in North America, Ireland and extensively in non-league football.

A LUCKY BREAK

Within 18 months of joining the Blades, goalkeeper Harry Gough had won an FA Cup winners' medal. However, despite the most inauspicious of debuts which saw him concede 4 to Tottenham, he remained the club's regular keeper for 7 seasons. However, had Ted Hafton, the recognised first choice between the sticks, not broken his nose, Gough may never have had the chance. The First World War cut into his early career but he remained number one either side of the conflict with Germany and her allies, making almost 300 appearances in the league and FA Cup. Cool, calm and collected were more than adequate descriptions of his style and he was one of the best men to have around the penalty area. He was also tough and possessed an ability to play the ball off either foot and gain large distances with clearances, which also marked him out from a number of his contemporaries. Others agreed and in the summer of 1920 he joined an FA tour to South Africa. A year later he won his only England cap when he played against Scotland at Hampden Park, but suffered a 3–0 defeat.

KEEPER TURNED TO DRINK

Harry Gough's decision to provide for himself outside the game cost the rewards his talents may have been expected to earn on the field. Less charitable souls may say playing behind a Blades defence during the 1910s would drive anyone to drink, but the running of a public house a decade after joining the club contravened his contract with United. While in dispute with his employers there was no chance of Gough joining any other League club. It created a stand-off as the keeper refused to give up his business interests and the Blades would not waive their conditions. Even the FA took action, removing Gough from the roster of players allowed to turn out in first-class competitions and many other lower levels of the game.

The decision was eventually reversed and although he continued to turn out for a number of amateur and semi-professional outfits, Gough could find no way back into the big-time due to the massive asking price. His last game was a cup-winning performance – a 2–0 County Cup win over Sheffield Wednesday at Hillsborough. A modest fee of £500 saw him finally break free and join Oldham Athletic.

MOONLIGHTING

Herbert Chapman	mining engineer
David White	who despite being valued at £1 million plus worked afternoons at his family's waste reclamation business
Neil Warnock	chiropodist, fruit and veg man

GOING WITH THE FLO

Former Blade Jostein Flo is one of very few players to have a move or specific tactic named after him. In Norwegian it is called 'Flopasning' – translated into English 'the Flo pass'. It gained prominence during a period of the early 1990s when the Scandinavians were ranked the world's second-best team and utilised a very basic ploy of a full-back, usually on the left, sending a long diagonal ball up to the totemic Flo. Though a striker, he would raid down the right using his height to his advantage by heading the ball on for a central midfielder or striker who knew their job was to dart through and test the opposing keeper. Something of a long-ball tactic eschewed by purists, it proved highly effective for a prolonged period as defences struggled to formulate a plan and is still used by many Norwegian clubs.

SEASON BY SEASON

To date United have spent 105 seasons in the Football or Premier League, of which 60 have been in the top flight. The longest run is the 37 campaigns from 1893 to 1934. Just 6 seasons have been outside the top two divisions, 5 in the old Third Division and just 1 in the old bottom rung then known as the Fourth Division. A 40th season on the second rung of the ladder was clocked up in August 2010.

UNBEATEN FROM THE START OF THE SEASON

Hopes of a title success were high when the Blades started the 1971/72 season with a 10-match unbeaten run. A point wasn't dropped until the fifth game when West Bromwich Albion came away from Bramall Lane with a goalless draw. Tottenham Hotspur were the only other team to deny Sheffield United maximum points but a 2–0 defeat at Old Trafford ended that run and precipitated a downward spiral; 13 defeats and 10 draws from the 32 games which remained led to a 10th place finish.

AFTER THE BALL

A look at some of the weird and wonderful occupations United players have taken after hanging up their boots. Not everyone runs a pub or becomes a coach:

Willie Falconer	sandwich shop owner
Terry Garbett	runs an office cleaning business in New York State
Gary Hamson	Liberal Democrat councillor in Erewash
Willie Hamilton	bricklayer
Mick Henderson	policeman
Jim Iley	restaurateur at an Italian eatery
Bert Lipsham	ran a tobacconist shop on Bramall Lane
John McAlle	landscape gardener
Ken McNaught	miner in Western Australia
Gil Reece	hotelier
Robert Ullathorne	lifestyle management coach

While many players turn out well into their middle age for a host of amateur or Sunday league sides, Wilf Rostron took to the field for perhaps the most interestingly named of them all after hanging up his boots at the age of 37. While coaching Gateshead United he donned a kit for a team called 'Oddies' in the Sunderland Catholic Club Over-40s league. Now that's the big-time!

BUYING AN ADVANTAGE

Although cup games can now only be switched to the ground of the team originally drawn out of the hat second (on police or safety advice), at one stage it was perfectly legitimate for the away team to buy home advantage. United struck one such deal with Bolton Wanderers in the second round of the 1889/90 FA Cup in exchange for £40. It seemed to be money well spent as far as the Lancashire club were concerned – they inflicted the worst ever defeat United have suffered and the final score was 13–0. Such practices are now completely outlawed by the FA.

IN THE DEEP MID-WINTER

Whole swathes of a season have been lost to the weather on 3 occasions. The first came during the Second World War when no play was possible from mid-January to early March due to heavy snowfall. The 1962/63 campaign was similarly decimated for just under a month, as snow and frozen pitches prevented any first-team games until the latter part of February.

During the harsh winter of 1899/1900 2 games were abandoned in the space of a month. The first was on 6 January against Blackburn Rovers when wind, rain and sleet combined to make the conditions unplayable. Officials were forced to call events to a halt after 36 minutes with the game delicately balanced at 0–0. The Sheffield derby in the second round of the FA Cup was the next victim on 10 February. Again the score was 0–0 when the game was abandoned 53 minutes in due to a heavy snowfall. The match was replayed seven days later and ended in a 1–1 draw. United eventually won through, courtesy of a 2–0 away win.

CAPTURING AN OLD MASTER

Although Ivor Allchurch's heyday was far behind him when he joined United in the early 1960s, his addition to the squad was a master stroke. The Blades were having trouble finding the net but the Welshman's addition precipitated a reversal in fortune making the £12,500 fee paid to Swansea Town seem very reasonable indeed. At the time of his signing, United had reached the last four of the FA Cup but the bid to reach the First Division seemed to be going off the rails. Rivals Ipswich Town had put themselves in the driving seat by beating the Blades, and other would-be candidates such as Liverpool, Norwich City and Middlesbrough were each enjoying decent runs of form. However, while Leicester went on to Wembley after three titanic games, Allchurch came in to his own, boosting the promotion cause with some great displays at outside-right. Added to this he scored on his debut in a 2–1 win over Leeds United at Elland Road, then scored another 4 goals in the 5 games that remained. Goalscoring had been a huge problem until that point but with the industrious and gifted ball-playing Allchurch, United always looked threatening in attack.

Over the next three seasons Bramall Lane played host to Allchurch's sublime skills which barely waned despite the player being in his 30s. Experience was a key factor in his contribution which, apart from the odd narrow squeak, ensured United remained among the English game's elite for a number of seasons. The Blades finished fifth in that initial campaign while the same team that pipped them to the divisional championship, Ipswich, won the Division One title. However, there was an awful lot for United to be proud of and once more Allchurch was at the heart of a lot of fine displays by the team. During his stint in Yorkshire, Allchurch had amassed almost 150 first-team outings.

A few weeks into the 1965/66 season he was allowed to join Stockport County where he went on to win the Fourth Division title. Three years later he won another promotion when he went back to his first league club, now known as Swansea City. He finished his playing days in the non-league scene with Haverfordwest and despite the buffeting he received from less skilled opponents throughout a career which spanned over 20 years, he was never so much as cautioned.

CLUBS AGREE SIX-FIGURE SUMS

In May 1975 Chris Guthrie became the first player signed for six figures courtesy of his £100,000 recruitment from Southend United. The Blades have set similar marks when selling players and in 1967 became the first club to sell a player for £100,000 or more. In fact, United parted company with not one but two players for this amount in quick succession when Mick Jones signed for Leeds United and Alan Birchenall signed for Chelsea.

At one stage during the late 1970s and early '80s, the same player was both the record fee paid out and then attracted the biggest fee ever received: Alex Sabella cost £160,000 when he came from River Plate just after the 1978 World Cup finals but Leeds United paid out £400,000 when they bought him just under two years later.

CLIMBING THE LEAGUE LADDER

After an entire career spent with Brentford, Bob Booker turned his back on football to earn his living as a window cleaner. That was at least until Dave Bassett tempted him back to the professional ranks with an offer to provide emergency cover for Simon Webster who had picked up a serious injury. He was thinking about going part-time with Barnet but, having turned 30 years of age, could not turn down the chance of one last fling before hanging up his boots. He took time to win the fans over but was a great header of the ball with strong enthusiasm and a physique to match. His temporary stay with the club turned out to be a somewhat longer odyssey than expected when the Blades were promoted to Division Two and then to Division One the following season.

Booker was the captain for the last game of the season when a vital 5–2 win over Leicester City finally secured automatic promotion and a place back among the elite. There is little doubt that these qualities played their part in United securing two successive promotions and Booker having an unexpected chance to sample life in the top flight for the first time. He played on over the next two seasons, although many of these appearances were from the bench. He left Bramall Lane in 1992 after United had achieved their best finish in 17 seasons. After 109 league and cup starts in which he scored 14 times, he returned to Brentford seeing out the remainder of his unexpectedly prolonged career.

SEEING DOUBLE

Two United players have earned supplementary income or post-retirement earnings by acting as a doppelgangers, though were not trying to pass themselves off as ropey look-a-likes. Clive Mendonca provided a body double in TV ads after hanging up his boots, while during his on-field career Ashley Sestanovich also provided body plus action double work for Thierry Henry's sponsorships with Nike and Renault. The French star's heavy insurance made certain demands from directors impossible to perform. There was far less fuss involved in the Lambeth-born midfielder throwing himself about.

AND FINALLY, DID YOU KNOW?

Paul Devlin was booked 11 times in his first full season at Bramall Lane. Though not the biggest number of yellow cards in a season, it earned the striker a lengthy suspension. Four cautions came in the last half-dozen games of that 1998/99 term.

Jostein Flo was a very good high-jumper during his youth and remains on his country's list of all-time best practitioners of the 'Fosbury Flop' with a leap of 2m 6cm in 1987.

In a Second Division game against Notts County, centre-half Jim Iley managed to miss 2 penalties within the space of just 4 minutes. Now that's a bad day at the office.

Sky Sports presenter and former Blade Chris Kamara often breathlessly shouts the catchphrase 'Unbelievable Jeff' to *Soccer Saturday* host Jeff Stelling when describing action during the course of games he is reporting on. The pair are coincidentally shareholders in a racehorse of the same name.